"If you are concerned that a loved one (or your flock) loves the Enneagram, let Rhenn Cherry's super-helpful book equip you to explain why the Enneagram should be an absolute no-go for Christians. *Enneagram Theology* is thorough, thoughtful, impeccably researched, and not hysterical and nasty. Lay people and preachers alike *need* to understand the underlying snares of the Enneagram. Rhenn meticulously exposes those snares."

—TODD FRIEL
Host of Wretched Radio and TV

"I was praying for a book like this. Rhenn really answers in a godly, loving, and well theologically based manner this tension that the use of the Enneagram brings to the body of Christ. Since my secular formation almost twenty years ago when I learned the Enneagram to recruit and select as a human resources student, and now that I'm seeing even pastors and churches use their pulpits to preach about it, I was deeply concerned about how this topic will affect the church. But with this book, Rhenn not only helps us to know why some leaders are using it, but also helps us to be aware of the risk of using it. If you are a pastor, a counselor, or a church member wanting to have a biblical perspective about the Enneagram, this book is for you."

—KIKE TORRES
Lead Pastor, Horizonte, Queretaro, Mexico

"Rhenn Cherry brings biblical exposition and philosophical inquiry together to explore the growing use of the Enneagram among Christians. While the Enneagram has enjoyed popularity among Evangelicals, Cherry points out that many who advocate for its use may be unaware of its theological moorings as expressed in the work of Richard Rohr. Through thoughtful and compelling research, this book does not ask *how* Christians should use the Enneagram, but *if* we should use it."

—SAMUEL E. STEPHENS
Assistant Professor of Biblical Counseling, Midwestern Baptist Theological Seminary

"A foundational consideration for Christians enthralled by or skeptical of the Enneagram is whether it is theologically sound. Rhenn Cherry's book *Enneagram Theology: Is it Christian?* answers that question with a resounding 'No!' This book will help you understand the background of the Enneagram and explore the theological and philosophical foundations that make it unbiblical. I heartily recommend it."

—JOHN E. BABLER

Professor and Chairman, Department of Biblical Counseling, Mid-America Baptist Theological Seminary

"There have been numerous times as a graduate professor and as a pastor that I have sought to find theologically insightful books that address contemporary issues facing the church and failed. Either they have been theologically simplistic or failed to address the real problem. *Enneagram Theology* is refreshingly different because it confronts a major problem in the church today with both theological acumen and problem-focused insight. Anyone who wishes to read a carefully reasoned book that probes significant fallacies in using the Enneagram for Christians, you must read this book! The 'spiritualized personality typology' the Enneagram promotes undermines biblical soteriology and anthropology for Christians and churches around the world. If you are a pastor or biblical counselor, this is a must-read. It will give you an extremely helpful theological tool for addressing this vital challenge for your church. I commend Rhenn Cherry for the careful work he has done!"

—JOHN D. STREET

Chair, Graduate Studies in Biblical Counseling, The Master's University and Seminary

"The Enneagram is promoted as an objective 'self-assessment tool.' But in this illuminating book, Rhenn Cherry shows that the Enneagram is anything but objective. Cherry's definitive analysis makes clear that Enneagram theology is grounded in the pluralistic panentheism of Richard Rohr, not the authoritative truth of God's Word. The Enneagram's corrupt foundation means that it is bad news. But Cherry has good news: instead of questing after our true self in gospel-denying mysticism, we can find our identity in the true human, Jesus Christ. This careful and readable book will help us do just that."

—OWEN STRACHAN

Provost and Research Professor of Theology, Grace Bible Theological Seminary

Enneagram Theology

Is It Christian?

Enneagram Theology

Is It Christian?

By
RHENN CHERRY

Foreword by
T. DALE JOHNSON, JR.

RESOURCE *Publications* · Eugene, Oregon

ENNEAGRAM THEOLOGY
Is It Christian?

Resource Publications
An Imprint of Wipf and Stock Publishers
199 W. 8th Ave., Suite 3
Eugene, OR 97401

www.wipfandstock.com

PAPERBACK ISBN: 978-1-6667-1595-8
HARDCOVER ISBN: 978-1-6667-1596-5
EBOOK ISBN: 978-1-6667-1597-2

08/12/21

To Terry, my wife,
my one flesh,
my helpmate.
You have given yourself
for Christ, for me,
and for so many others.
You are without equal
in devotion and faithfulness.
I love you and honor you.

To Carly and Jack,
You are a heritage from the Lord.
God is so very good.

Contents

Foreword

I remember the series of discussions that led Rhenn to write on the Enneagram. As many of my students have done, he was asking for advice about dissertation topics. The meandering back and forth of those conversations landed on an assessment of personality typologies. Rhenn was most familiar at the time with the Myers-Briggs Personality Type Indicator (MBTI). He and his family had served as missionaries, and the MBTI was used during their candidacy as an evaluative tool. I could tell that Rhenn's interest was piqued by the topic based on his own personal experience.

The popular acceptance of personality typologies has long been a concern of mine. I thought it would be a good idea to have Rhenn present research with theological analysis to aid believers in thinking biblically about these intriguing tools. In our early discussions, Rhenn wanted to look at the MBTI, specifically exploring the influence of Freud's disciple Carl Jung on Katherine Briggs and her daughter Isabel Myers. The roots of Jungian theory in the Myers-Briggs was intriguing to me, especially since many Christian organizations have adopted the MBTI as a means of assessment believing it is useful for issues like conflict management. He would need to not only look at the theological aspects, but also assess whether or not these typologies were validated by scientific inquiry.

The lack of scientific support consistently demonstrated with personality typologies is due in large part to the subjective nature of the testing. Self-reporting can become a self-fulfilling prophecy. People who are ambitious tend to answer personality type questions based upon who they want to become, which is a jaded assessment of who they are now. Folks who are more self-deprecating tend to answer based on the idea that they can never be the person they wish they were. Personality self-assessment can be jaded and fickle depending upon so many variables, which is one reason that makes their outcomes questionable as *science.*

But before we settled on the MBTI, I was a little concerned that its popularity had been waning. While it is still used in various segments of the population, personality typologies generally have a faddish nature to them, moving in and out of vogue. You may be familiar with the Myers-Briggs or some of the other tests like the Minnesota Multiphasic Personality Inventory-2 (MMPI-2), DiSC, or the Rorschach Inkblot. Many of these personality typologies, like the MBTI, are used in various settings like counseling, hiring decisions, and conflict management in a team environment.

Rhenn needed to research something that was related specifically to the evangelical world. While many of the above personality tests have been used and could even be considered popular with evangelicals, I had been hearing about another typology which seemed to be growing in popularity within evangelical circles. I did not know a great deal about the Enneagram, at the time, but had read several articles and continued to hear of its use in various Christian contexts. I was like so many other pastors and administrators who are busy and have probably not been able to give much attention to researching the theological details that create the foundations of the Enneagram. Our tendency toward pragmatism makes us more vulnerable to a tool like the Enneagram. Christian leaders are especially vulnerable when we are not aware of overt breaches to our doctrinal stances based on our surface understanding of a tool like the Enneagram. In fact, our default is often that we do not want to keep people away from something they may find helpful without first considering some of the underlying philosophies that may be compromising the doctrines we hold dear. We have little time to sincerely vet every faddish tool that arises, so we will either endorse it by our silence or we will acknowledge a usefulness of the tool because of its popularity and seeming benefit.

The gravitational pull of the Enneagram and its newly found fame within evangelicalism is rooted in its clear and concise explanations of human personality. We are always drawn to tools that attempt to organize and explain elements of our world that seem otherwise mysterious. Personality labels and descriptions make us to feel like we have mastered some part of knowledge that seems out of reach. Our human desire to have objective means to explain or understand ourselves increases our vulnerability to these forms of gnostic insight. "The heart is deceitful above all things, and desperately sick, who can understand it?" (Jeremiah 17:9) If we are all honest, we know how flawed our self-interpretations can be. Biblically, however, the only way we understand the type of person we are is not by our own judgments and not by cultural wisdom.

The Bible is clear that it is the Holy Spirit who unveils and helps us to see the type of person we are. He illuminates the heart (2 Corinthians 3). We also see in James 1:25 that our deep gaze into the perfect law of liberty helps us see the type of person we really are. The Bible tells us if we walk away from that, if we're not a doer of the Word, we forget the type of person we are. It is the Word of Christ dwelling in us richly that exposes us (Hebrews 4:12–13).

These tests are often man's attempt to reduce himself from a complex changing—sometimes even conflicting—person into a neat category. Personality tests typically produce results in the forms of labeling an individual. Each test usually has its own unique vocabulary for describing who people are according to that particular system. It does not negate the fact that the subjectivity involved in these typologies can only be classified as pseudoscience.

The power of the pseudoscience is found in the sense of self-awareness we feel by the descriptive labels that give context to our human experience. Further, there is an assumption that we can self-regulate when we become self-aware. Self-awareness is sort of step one in our ability to change, as if it starts the mechanism to empower self-regulation. There are two apparent flaws here. First, that we can be made *self-aware* without the work of the Holy Spirit through God's Word. Second, the assumption that we can *self-regulate*. Is this really just a different gospel challenging a biblical view of the Holy Spirit and sanctification?

This is where Dr. Jay Adams started in the 1970s, where he recognized that we are either missing the role of the Holy Spirit or trying to offer something as a substitute in his place. Personality tests attempt to build a system that helps us to know and understand ourselves in terms of explanatory details and labels that are outside the work of the Holy Spirit. For Christians, this should at least raise caution because it's redefining the work that the Bible clearly ascribes to the Holy Spirit.

In the end, personality typing and testing makes swift judgments about people. Trained experts, or the tests themselves, serve as the authority to assign people a label and a group. These labels and these groups are often welcomed by the people who take the test. There is a danger in believing that because you have labeled a person, you therefore understand that person, including yourself. What may be even more concerning is the illusion that self-mastery comes from self-knowledge according to a man-made system.

I think we can all agree that the Enneagram is currently the most popular self-knowledge tool utilized among Christians. The popularity of the Enneagram demands our attention. While it is similar to many of the previous personality typologies, it is different because it is marketed as a spiritual tool infused with ancient wisdom, which makes it particularly enticing to many.

After several more discussions, we landed on Rhenn's exploration of the Enneagram. The fruit of his labor can be a service to the many pastors and administrators who have been too busy in ministry to properly assess this popular tool. It has been an enjoyable journey walking with Rhenn through this project, and I am grateful that you now can benefit from the work he has done to help us think biblically about the Enneagram.

T. Dale Johnson, Jr.
Associate Professor of Biblical Counseling at Midwestern Baptist Theological Seminary
Executive Director, The Association of Certified Biblical Counselors

Acknowledgements

The Lord is ever faithful to provide all that you need to complete the things that he calls you to do. The endeavor of completing a book can be isolating at times, but the work is never truly accomplished alone. I am so very thankful for all those who prayed for me and helped me along the way. During this process, God showed me places in my own heart that I did not know existed, and he chiseled many of those parts away, to the glory of his name. Thank you, Lord Jesus, for your faithfulness.

I would like to express my gratitude to Dr. Dale Johnson, who stretched me beyond my personal limits while guiding me and encouraging me. I am thankful for your leadership and the persistent walk with Christ that you model so well. You and your family have been such a blessing to me and my family. You are a true Brother in Christ, and I love suiting up and going into battle alongside you. Dr. John Babler challenged me to be an "owner of the field" and taught me to evaluate everything that I encounter through the lens of Scripture. Dr. Frank Catanzaro pastored me and taught me not to be intimidated by sophisticated philosophies or pseudo-scientific diagnoses offered by the world. I am thankful for your sincere desire to see truth proclaimed. As someone who recently walked this same road, Dr. Sam Stephens gave me encouragement to persevere during some difficult times. He prayed for me earnestly and inspired me to finish strong. You are my Brother in the Fight, and I am so very thankful for your friendship.

I give God alone the credit and glory for my family. I stand amazed that the Lord has redeemed us and enabled us to love each other the way we do. I am so very thankful that he allows us to do life on this earth together. Your handwritten notes, texts, and phone calls encouraged me along the way and helped me refocus on the Lord when I needed to do so. Carly and Jack, you both demonstrate your faith in Christ in different ways that would encourage any father, and I rest knowing that you submit yourselves to the work of the King. I pray that God will continue to use you in a mighty way for the glory of his name. I am so very proud of you both. Terry, my wife, I am humbled by the selfless love you demonstrate for me, our children, and so many others. You are the most loyal and faithful person I have ever known. You endured my late nights and absences from home so that I could finish this project, and you encouraged me and covered me with prayer along the way. Thank you for your patience and endurance. This work is very much ours together. I delight in you, and I thank the Lord that you are mine. To God be the glory!

Rhenn Cherry
Kansas City, Missouri
April 2021

Introduction

The Enneagram has become popular among evangelical Christians as a spiritualized personality typology that claims to help people better understand themselves and others. Several influential evangelical Christian leadership ministries have promoted the Enneagram as a tool in forming and maintaining effective ministry teams, and the personality typology has been taught and embraced at several Christian universities and seminaries. Although the Enneagram is now utilized by individuals, churches, and Christian institutions for various purposes, some remain uncertain about whether it is appropriate to refer to the Enneagram as a Christian tool. Are pastors and Christian institutional leaders aware of the theology associated with the Enneagram?

Richard Rohr is a Catholic priest and popular author who has influenced several Enneagram authors popular among evangelicals. Rohr has taught a panentheism based on a belief that the first of multiple incarnations occurred at creation and that all of mankind is already "in Christ." He has also taught that man is good by nature and that original sin is a burdensome mental construct popularized by Augustine in the fifth century. Rohr has also maintained that multiple paths exist to God and that no one religion can claim to have knowledge of an exclusive way of salvation for man. But these doctrinal claims of Rohr are in conflict with orthodox evangelical theology.

Enneagram Theology: Is It Christian? documents the theology and anthropology that Richard Rohr demonstrated in his theological and Enneagram works, then goes on to compare Rohr's doctrines of God and man with an orthodox evangelical theology and anthropology. The book then traces a line of influence from Richard Rohr to Enneagram authors Ian Cron, Suzanne Stabile, and Christopher Heuertz. From there, *Enneagram Theology* demonstrates the impact of Enneagram authors Cron, Stabile, and

Heuertz on evangelical universities, Christian leadership ministries, and historically evangelical publishers.

Enneagram Theology confirms, based on the theological and anthropological doctrines taught by Richard Rohr which are in conflict with orthodox evangelical theology and anthropology, that the Enneagram should be abandoned and rejected as non-Christian. This book raises this question: Can Rohr's panentheism and multiple paths to God ever be accurately labeled as Christian when they deny so many of the core doctrines of the Bible? The Enneagram presents a dangerous shift in focus away from the holiness of the God of the Bible and toward the discovery of a mythical good True Self that does not exist. The Enneagram also poses the danger of mischaracterizing man's problem as one of mistaken identity rather than total depravity, and the Enneagram solution of self-knowledge represents a false gospel. The Enneagram version of the restoration of man looks like reconnection with his original good True Self. *Enneagram Theology: Is It Christian?* concludes by affirming that Christians who hold to an orthodox theology are called to separate themselves from heretical teaching like Richard Rohr's theology and anthropology, in spite of the sincere motives of some evangelicals to help others by teaching the Enneagram.

The Enneagram has been widely promoted as an ancient personality typing tool, and the claim that it contains "spiritual wisdom" has contributed to its increasing popularity in evangelical churches.[1] The Enneagram symbol itself is distinct from the personality labels that proponents have overlaid onto its nine points over the last fifty years.[2] The Enneagram's history reveals that while the symbol itself has a somewhat mysterious origin, secular psychiatrists in the 1970s are responsible for developing and applying the symbol's nine personality types.[3] It was during that period

1. Katherine Burgess, "The Enneagram Is Taking Off among Christians: It's a Tool That Maps Out People's Nine Personality Types," *The Commercial Appeal*, February 16, 2020, https://www.commercialappeal.com/story/life/2020/02/04/why-enneagram-type-test-popular-with-christians/4600988002/; Jana Riess, "Why Has the Enneagram Become So Popular among Christians?," *Religion News Service*, July 11, 2018, https://religionnews.com/2018/07/11/why-has-the-enneagram-become-so-popular-among-christians/; Christopher L. Heuertz, *The Sacred Enneagram: Finding Your Unique Path to Spiritual Growth* (Grand Rapids: Zondervan, 2017), 25, 43-44; Don Richard Riso, and Russ Hudson, *The Wisdom of the Enneagram: The Complete Guide to Psychological and Spiritual Growth for the Nine Personality Types* (New York: Bantam Books, 1999), 19.

2. Riso and Hudson, *Wisdom*, 19-20; Heuertz, *Sacred*, 47-48.

3. Carolyn Bartlett, "Viewing Therapy through a New Lens," *Annals Of The American Psychotherapy Association* 11, no. 1 (2008): 34.

that the personality typologies, known as Ennea-types, were assigned to each point on the symbol.[4] Roman Catholic Jesuits became students of the Enneagram, propagated its use at seminaries and spiritual retreats, and endorsed it as a tool for effecting personal change.[5] Father Richard Rohr, a Catholic priest and popular Enneagram author and speaker, has influenced several best-selling Enneagram writers who are popular among evangelicals.[6] Evangelical authors Don and Joy Veinot and Marcia Montenegro have noted Rohr's influence on evangelicalism, stating, "One cannot disconnect the Enneagram from Richard Rohr, which is why it is essential to know his beliefs, especially since the writers of the two main [Enneagram] books in use among evangelicals are his students and have taught at his Center for Action and Contemplation (CAC)."[7]

Given Richard Rohr's influence on evangelicalism, should Christians have concerns about the foundational theology and anthropology Rohr demonstrates in his theological and Enneagram works? Does use of the Enneagram lead to a non-Christian way of viewing man and understanding man's problems? These concerns confirm that an evaluation of Rohr's theology and anthropology is warranted and necessary in order to determine whether the Enneagram is an appropriate biblical tool for use by evangelical Christians.

Summary of Chapter Contents

The first chapter will provide background information on the Enneagram and Richard Rohr before introducing the general issues of Rohr's panentheistic theology and perennial philosophy. Then the following specific research question will be raised: Based on an analysis of Richard Rohr's

4. Claudio Naranjo, *Ennea-Type Structures: Self-Analysis for the Seeker* (Nevada City, CA: Gateways Publishers, 1990).

5. Richard Rohr and Andreas Ebert, *The Enneagram: A Christian Perspective* (New York: Crossroad Publishing, 2018), 20; Heuertz, *Sacred*, 48–49.

6. Ian Morgan Cron, and Suzanne Stabile, *The Road Back to You: An Enneagram Journey to Self-Discovery* (Downers Grove, IL: InterVarsity, 2016), 19; Heuertz, *Sacred*, 9–11; Suzanne Stabile, *The Path in Between Us: An Enneagram Journey to Healthy Relationships* (Downers Grove, IL: InterVarsity Press, 2018), 186.

7. Don Veinot, Joy Veinot, and Marcia Montenegro, *Richard Rohr and the Enneagram Secret* (Wonder Lake, IL: MCOI Publishing, 2020), 26. Veinot and Montenegro refer to Ian Cron and Suzanne Stabile's *The Road Back to You* and Christopher Heuertz's *The Sacred Enneagram* as the two main Enneagram books in use among evangelicals.

theological and anthropological influence on Enneagram authors Ian Cron, Suzanne Stabile, and Christopher Heuertz, who are popular among evangelical Christians, should the Enneagram be accepted as an appropriate Christian tool among evangelical Christians? This chapter will demonstrate why a study of Rohr's panentheistic theology and perennial philosophy is beneficial to evangelical Christians and institutions. Then the chapter will provide definitions for the terms "orthodoxy and orthodox," "evangelicalism and evangelical," "incarnation," "panentheism," and "perennial philosophy." Next, a literature review will include Rohr's theological and Enneagram works as well as works by Enneagram authors Cron, Stabile, and Heuertz. The works of several theologians and commentators who are representative of an orthodox evangelical theology and anthropology will be briefly reviewed. These representative orthodox evangelical theological works will be utilized to evaluate Rohr's claim that a first incarnation occurred at creation—as well as Rohr's claim that all of creation is already "in Christ." Chapter 1 will conclude with a brief summary of Enneagram history and raises questions for readers to consider as Enneagram theology is evaluated throughout this work.

Chapter 2 will begin with an overview of Richard Rohr's panentheistic theology and then identify two claims that he uses to support his panentheism. First, analysis of references and quotes by Rohr will demonstrate his commitment to panentheistic theology. Next, evidence from Rohr's own theological works will reveal his proposition that the first incarnation occurred at creation. This chapter will evaluate "incarnation" from the works of several systematic theologians who are representative of an orthodox evangelical theology before establishing and explaining Rohr's interpretation and application of "in Christ" as he uses it to support his claim that all of creation has already been united with God. Finally, the works of representative orthodox evangelical commentators will provide an interpretation of four scriptural passages to which Rohr appeals for support of his "in Christ" claim. Chapter 2 will conclude with a summary of the foundational claims that support Rohr's panentheism as well as a summary of an orthodox evangelical response to the notion of a first incarnation occurring at creation and an all-inclusive interpretation of "in Christ."

Chapter 3 will examine Richard Rohr's anthropology and perennial philosophy. First, Rohr's anthropology will be presented as a product of his panentheistic theology, and further analysis will demonstrate that Rohr's claim of all things, including man, being "in Christ" at the first incarnation results in an anthropological presupposition that man is basically good. Corollary to his doctrine that man is basically good is Rohr's proposed solution for man of using the Enneagram as a tool to discover his good True Self. Rohr's anthropological influence on Cron, Stabile, and Heuertz will become evident through their extensive use of the term True Self to describe the self-knowledge solution made possible by the Enneagram. In response to Rohr's anthropology, this chapter will present an orthodox evangelical anthropology that highlights man's sinful nature and need for salvation, demonstrated through several representative evangelical Christian authors. The second part of chapter 3 will focus on Rohr's perennial philosophy, which acknowledges multiple paths to God. Rohr's commitment to the modern perennialism popularized by Aldous Huxley will be demonstrated by Rohr's endorsement of multiple paths to God in his own Enneagram works as well as in the works of authors he mentored and influenced. Chapter 3 will conclude with an orthodox evangelical doctrine of the exclusive claim that Christ is the one way to salvation and that the Bible, not the Enneagram, is God's chosen tool to guide man.

Chapter 4 will examine the relationships that Richard Rohr has developed with Enneagram authors Ian Cron, Suzanne Stabile, and Christopher Heuertz, demonstrating the impact that his teaching and mentoring has had on each of them. This chapter will then show the different ways in which Cron, Stabile, and Heuertz have each influenced evangelicalism. Specific attention will be given to evaluating their influence on evangelical Christianity in the areas of leadership training, higher education, and evangelical publishing. The Enneagram works of two couples, the McCords and Gaultieres, whom Rohr did *not* mentor, will be evaluated briefly to see how they promote Richard Rohr and his works. Chapter 4 will conclude with a summary and comparison of how each Enneagram author has influenced evangelicalism.

Chapter 5 is the conclusion and will summarize the panentheistic theology and perennial philosophy of Richard Rohr as demonstrated in his own theological and Enneagram works as well as in the works of Enneagram authors whom Rohr has influenced. The conclusion will go on to review reasons for concern about use of the Enneagram among evangelical Christians, summarizing areas of potential confusion and deception. An untenable contradiction between the Enneagram and orthodox evangelical theology and anthropology will be demonstrated to substantiate a call for churches and Christian leaders to avoid, abandon, and reject the use of the Enneagram. This work will conclude with the identification and submission of further areas of research with the hope that other scholars will pursue them.

Conclusion

The goal of *Enneagram Theology: Is It Christian?* is to answer the following research question: Based on an analysis of Richard Rohr's theological and anthropological influence on Enneagram authors Ian Cron, Suzanne Stabile, and Christopher Heuertz and their popularity among evangelical Christians, should the Enneagram be accepted as an appropriate biblical tool among evangelical Christians? The following chapters will document and evaluate Richard Rohr's panentheistic theology and perennial philosophy after an examination of his written theological and Enneagram works. The evidence will confirm that Richard Rohr's panentheistic theology and anthropology, as well as that of Ian Cron, Suzanne Stabile, and Christopher Heuertz, are inconsistent with orthodox evangelical theology and anthropology. Therefore, the Enneagram should be considered unbiblical and rejected for use within churches and Christian institutions alike.

1

Background, Important Terms, and Influential Relationships

The term Enneagram comes from a combination of the Greek words εννεα, meaning "nine," and γραμμα, meaning "that which is written or drawn."[1] The Enneagram symbol consists of a circle with nine points located on the circle's circumference.[2] Explaining the *origin* of the Enneagram, however, is not so straightforward. There is no general agreement on the source or date of origin of the Enneagram symbol, but possible dates of origin range from Babylonian times to as late as the sixteenth century.[3] Some

1. Thayer, *Greek-English Lexicon*, 120.

2. The numeral 9 is positioned at the highest point on the circle's circumference. The other eight numerals, beginning with 1, are located sequentially clockwise from the 9. The inside of the circle consists of an equilateral triangle formed by internally connecting points 9, 3, and 6. The remaining six circumferential points are connected internally in the order determined by the mathematical quotient of the number 1 divided by 7, which is the series of numerals 1, 4, 2, 8, 5, and 7 in that distinct infinite order. Interestingly, any cardinal number divided by the number seven yields a quotient with a remainder consisting of those same six numbers in the same ongoing infinite sequence. For example, 1 divided by $7 = 0.142857142857142857\ldots$. The series of six numerals 142857 continues infinitely. This infinitely repeating sequence of numbers, referred to as a "repetend," can be designated mathematically as $0.(142857)$. Similarly, 2 divided by $7 = 0.(285714)$, 3 divided by $7 = 0.(428571)$, and so on.

3. Heuertz, *Sacred*, 42–44; Riso and Hudson, *Wisdom*, 19; Fryling, *Mirror for the Soul*, 8. Alice Fryling, a popular author on Christian application of the Enneagram, claims "We know that the Christian roots of the Enneagram probably go back to the desert mothers and fathers of the fourth century. They are often considered the 'spiritual directors' or mentors of the early church. As people sought them out for help on the spiritual journey,

credit the Sufi Muslims of Central Asia with developing the Enneagram symbol between the thirteenth and sixteenth centuries.[4] But there is little dispute that the Enneagram *symbol* was introduced to the Western world in the early 1900s by G. I. Gurdjieff, who became familiar with it while in Afghanistan.[5] Gurdjieff used the Enneagram to teach his students mysterious "esoteric subjects," which apparently did not include any psychological or personality typology.[6]

During the 1950s and 1960s, a Bolivian named Oscar Ichazo developed an application of the Enneagram symbol in relation to human personality, claiming to have learned it from Afghani Sufi masters before he came upon Gurdjieff's writings on the subject.[7] Ichazo's work with the Enneagram symbol was part of a larger body of work he called "protoanalysis," which focused on the human being as a whole.[8] His teaching was a mixture of methods aimed at achieving higher levels of consciousness and "full enlightenment," which included studying astrological signs, mantras, and physical organs and systems of the human body.[9] Claudio Naranjo, a Fulbright scholar and Gestalt psychiatrist, studied protoanalysis with Ichazo and brought it to the United States in the early 1970s. Naranjo wanted to utilize the term "protoanalysis" to describe his own work and teaching on

---

these teachers saw patterns of life that are reflected in the Enneagram." But Fryling's claim of Christian roots for the Enneagram is unsubstantiated, without any reference or supporting footnote.

4. Wagner and Walker, "Reliability and Validity Study," 712; Rohr and Ebert, *Discovering*, 5–7; Heuertz, *Sacred*, 44.

5. Riso and Hudson, *Wisdom*, 20; Rohr and Ebert, *Discovering*, 8; Heuertz, *Sacred*, 47.

6. Cron and Stabile, *Road*, 10; Ellis, Abrams, and Abrams, *Personality Theories*, 571; Rohr and Ebert, *Discovering*, 8–9; Riso and Hudson, *Wisdom*, 20. According to Heuertz, Gurdjieff developed a more universal understanding of the Enneagram, believing that it could be used "as an overlay to explain any evolved system, be it religion, science, or astrology," Heuertz, *Sacred*, 45. Ouspensky studied under Gurdjieff and maintained that Gurdjieff believed that "Everything can be included and read in the Enneagram," Ouspensky, *In Search*, 294.

7. Rohr and Ebert, *Discovering*, 9.

8. Naranjo, *Ennea-Type Structures*, 1–3, 156.

9. Riso, *Personality Types*, 16; Ellis, Abrams, and Abrams, *Personality Theories*, 571–72; Riso and Hudson, *Wisdom*, 22–24. Eventually, Ichazo developed and characterized his nine psychological types as "ego fixations" in an effort to bring his labels more into agreement with the modern psychology of his day.

personality typology, but because Ichazo had trademarked the term, Naranjo instead coined the term "Ennea-types."[10]

In the 1960s, Naranjo studied under Fritz Perls to learn Gestalt therapy, "an experiential therapy stressing awareness and integration [which] grew as a reaction against analytic therapy."[11] Naranjo eventually combined Perls's psychiatry with Ichazo's protoanalysis and overlaid the nine Ennea-types onto the Enneagram symbol. Ichazo's protoanalysis and Naranjo's Ennea-types combined with Perls's Gestalt psychiatry to form the foundation for most modern Enneagram psychological profiling systems and tests.[12] Naranjo began teaching the Ennea-types at the Esalen Institute in Big Sur, California, in the early 1970s.[13] One of Naranjo's students, an American Jesuit priest named Robert Ochs, began adapting his own handwritten notes on the Ennea-types to meet Catholic spiritual formation and counseling needs for seminarians and laypeople.[14] By 1974, Enneagram materials for use at Jesuit retreats had developed into one-page sketches of the nine different personality types. Those pages became the foundational ideas of a Jesuit seminarian, Don Riso, and a Franciscan priest, Richard Rohr. Riso would go on to write the formative work *Personality Types* in 1987, and Rohr wrote *Discovering the Enneagram* in 1989.[15] Both men and their works are considered seminal in the further development of Enneagram books, seminars, and personality tests.[16]

---

10. Naranjo, *Ennea-Type Structures*, 1–3.

11. Corey, *Theory and Practice*, 9, 198–227.

12. Riso, *Personality Types*, 17; Rohr and Ebert, *Discovering*, 9; Heuertz, *Sacred*, 47–48.

13. Ellis, Abrams, and Abrams, *Personality Theories*, 572; Riso, *Personality Types*, 17; Rohr and Ebert, *Discovering*, 9. The Esalen Institute is a non-profit founded in 1962. "Esalen is a major catalyst in the transformation of humankind, working with individuals and institutions to integrate body, mind, heart, spirit, and community in a nurturing relationship with the environment." "Our Mission & Values," Esalen.

14. Heuertz, *Sacred*, 48; Riso, *Personality Types*, 17; Rohr and Ebert, *Discovering*, 9. Although Robert Ochs never published material on the Ennea-types, he was instrumental in teaching this personality typology at Jesuit theological centers such as Loyola University in Chicago and the University of California at Berkeley.

15. Riso, *Personality Types*, 16–17; Rohr and Ebert, *Discovering the Enneagram* was first published as *Das Enneagram: Die 9 Gesichter der Seele* in 1989 and translated in 1990.

16. Cron, Stabile, and Heuertz acknowledge both Rohr and Riso, and their respective books, as formative and influential in helping them develop their own Enneagram works.

Enneagram Theology: Is It Christian? will focus on the theological and Enneagram works of Richard Rohr and the works of three Enneagram authors whom Rohr has influenced.[17] Rohr has personally mentored Ian Cron, Suzanne Stabile, and Christopher Heuertz, who have each published their own Enneagram works that are popular among evangelicals.[18] Like Rohr, these three Enneagram authors have developed large followings as best-selling authors and speakers, and their impact in the evangelical community has become significant.[19]

Richard Rohr has advocated and defended a panentheistic theology that consists of two foundational components. The first core element of Rohr's panentheism is a dogma that the first incarnation occurred at creation.[20] Rohr has maintained that God indwelled all of creation at the actual event of creation; therefore, all of creation has a divine nature. The second primary component of Rohr's panentheism is his interpretation of "in Christ." Rohr has interpreted the biblical term "in Christ" to mean that all of creation—including humanity—is already divine in nature.[21] Rohr's belief that a first incarnation occurred at creation has combined with his belief that all of creation is already "in Christ" to produce an anthropological presupposition that man is good and divine in nature.[22] According to Rohr, man's problem reduces to a need to discover his hidden—but good—True Self, which has always existed from creation.[23] Rohr and the Enneagram authors whom he has influenced have promoted the Enneagram as the perfect tool to help people discover their True Selves.[24]

Richard Rohr has also embraced and promoted a modern perennial philosophy that was popularized by Aldous Huxley's work *The Perennial Philosophy*.[25] To Huxley and his followers, this perennial philosophy ad-

17. Cron and Stabile, *Road*; Heuertz, *Sacred*. Cron, Stabile, and Heuertz acknowledge and quote Rohr in their works.

18. Cron and Stabile, *Road*, 19; Heuertz, *Sacred*, 9–11; Stabile, *Path*, 186.

19. DeWaay, *Enneagram*, Kindle, location 28; Veinot, Veinot, and Montenegro, *Richard Rohr*, 22, 26.

20. Rohr, *Universal*, 12, 16, 20–22.

21. Rohr, *Universal*, 43–46.

22. Rohr, *Universal*, 55–68.

23. Rohr, *Divine*, vii–viii, xiii, 1–26; Rohr and Ebert, *Christian*, xvi–xvii; 4–5; Rohr, *Universal*, 25–37.

24. Rohr and Ebert, *Christian*, ix–xxiii; Rohr and Ebert, *Experiencing*, 3–14.

25. Huxley, *Perennial Philosophy*. For articles that Rohr has written to demonstrate his commitment to a perennial philosophy, see "The Perennial Tradition," Center for

vocates that "the content of the world's major religions and mystical traditions can be reduced to certain common principles, which together make up the 'philosophy' they propose to call 'perennial'" due to its recurrence throughout history in all major religions.[26] The perennialism popularized by Huxley and advanced by Rohr acknowledges multiple paths to God.[27] Because the Enneagram promoted by Rohr and the authors he has influenced provides nine paths to finding one's good True Self and God, it fits well with a perennial philosophy that acknowledges multiple paths to the same God.[28]

Richard Rohr's theological and anthropological influence on Ian Cron, Suzanne Stabile, and Christopher Heuertz is evident in their own extensive use of the term True Self to describe a person's good, divine identity, which the Enneagram enables them to discover.[29] Rohr uses the term True Self throughout his theological works *The Universal Christ*, *Immortal Diamond*, and *The Divine Dance* as well as in his Enneagram works *Discovering the Enneagram* and *The Enneagram: A Christian Perspective* to describe the divine nature that all mankind received at the first incarnation, which occurred at creation.[30]

But an analysis of Richard Rohr's theology and anthropology, as well as how these doctrines have influenced these three Enneagram authors, is needed to help evangelicals make an informed decision about the appropriateness of using the Enneagram in the church. Therefore, a comparison of Rohr's influential theology and anthropology with an orthodox evangelical theology and anthropology will be helpful in determining whether the Enneagram is appropriate for evangelical Christians to use. *Enneagram Theology: Is It Christian?* provides this needed analysis.

Action and Contemplation; "Interfaith Friendship," Center for Action and Contemplation; and "Perennial Wisdom," Center for Action and Contemplation. Rohr quotes and paraphrases Huxley extensively in his own articles on perennialism.

26. Carlson, *Words of Wisdom*, 153–54.

27. Cutsinger, "Christianity and Perennial Philosophy," 912–14.

28. Rohr and Ebert, *Christian*, xvii, 4–5, 48, 201, 228; Cron and Stabile, *Road*, 23–24, 31, 34, 230; Heuertz, *Sacred*, 11, 15, 22–23, 25–27, 31–32, 37, 39, 43, 53.

29. Examples of Enneagram authors using the term True Self can be found in the following locations: Rohr and Ebert, *Christian*, xvii, 4–5, 48, 201, 228; Cron and Stabile, *Road*, 23–24, 31, 34, 230; Heuertz, *Sacred*, 11, 15, 22–23, 25–27, 31–32, 37, 39, 43, 53. These references to each author's use of the term True Self in their Enneagram works is not represented as their only uses of the term.

30. Rohr, *Immortal*, vii–viii, x–xiv, xvi, xxii. Rohr titled the first chapter of *Immortal Diamond* "What is the 'True Self?'" Rohr, *Universal*, 12, 16, 20–22.

A Research Question

Based on an analysis of Richard Rohr's theological and anthropological influence on Enneagram authors Ian Cron, Suzanne Stabile, and Christopher Heuertz and their popularity among evangelical Christians, should evangelical Christians accept the Enneagram as an appropriate Christian tool? This question has arisen due to the increased popularity and level of influence that the Enneagram now has among evangelical Christian publishers, institutions, and churches.[31] *Enneagram Theology: Is It Christian?* demonstrates that Richard Rohr's claim that the Enneagram is a useful Christian tool is based on a panentheistic theology and a perennial philosophy which are contrary to orthodox evangelical theology and anthropology. Therefore, as a result of this conflicting theology and anthropology, the Enneagram should be rejected by evangelical Christians as an unbiblical tool. In order to most effectively frame out this discussion, I will provide working definitions of certain terms that will be used throughout this book.

Definition of Important Terms

Orthodoxy and Orthodox

The terms orthodoxy and orthodox have various meanings. They can describe a measure of conformity to an established standard or body of knowledge and practice, or the actual Eastern Orthodox branch of Christianity, or a member of the Orthodox church.[32] In this book, the author will utilize J. I. Packer's definition of orthodoxy as "right belief, as opposed to heresy or heterodoxy. The word [orthodoxy] expresses the idea that certain statements accurately embody Christianity's revealed truth content and are therefore in their own nature normative for the universal church."[33]

---

31. Merritt, "What Is the 'Enneagram,'"; Burgess, "Enneagram Is Taking Off"; Riess, "Enneagram So Popular"; Veinot, Veinot, and Montenegro, *Richard Rohr*, 22, 26.

32. *Oxford English Dictionary*, 951; *Shorter Oxford English Dictionary*, 2025; *Merriam-Webster's Collegiate Dictionary*, 876.

33. Packer, "Orthodoxy," 631.

Evangelicalism and Evangelical

Much confusion exists over the precise meanings of evangelicalism and evangelical.[34] The terms have been used to describe a variety of concepts, such as historical renewal movements, or an adherence to certain key doctrines, or a tradition within Protestant Christianity.[35] In this book, the author will employ Kenneth Keathley's characterization of the evangelical commitment to the message of salvation found in the Bible as evangelicalism's defining trait: "God has planned and provided salvation through his Son, Jesus Christ, and all people are called to repentance from sin and to faith in his finished work."[36] Theological doctrine that is consistent with this defining trait will be considered evangelical in this work.

Incarnation

This book will utilize the definition of incarnation from R. L. Reymond in the *Evangelical Dictionary of Theology* as "the act whereby the eternal Son of God, the Second Person of the Holy Trinity, without ceasing to be what he is, God the Son, took into union with himself what he before that act did not possess, a human nature and so [he] was and continues to be God and man in two distinct natures and one person, forever."[37]

Panentheism

Panentheism has been referred to as a distinct "middle position between theism and pantheism."[38] This book will utilize a more thorough definition from *The New Dictionary of Theology*:

> Panentheism is the view that the universe is God, though God is more than the universe. It should be clearly distinguished from

34. Monsma, "What Is an Evangelical?," 323.

35. Monsma, "What Is an Evangelical?," 324–34.

36. Keathley, "Work of God: Salvation," 553. Keathley is Senior Professor of Theology at Southeastern Baptist Theological Seminary.

37. Reymond, "Incarnation," 424. Reymond presents his definition of *incarnation* and states that "Scripture's support for this doctrine [of *incarnation*] is replete—for example, John 1:14; Romans 1:3–4; 8:3; Galatians 4:4; Philippians 2:6–8; 1 Timothy 3:16; 1 John 4:2; 2 John 7."

38. Drees, "Panentheism and Natural Science," 1063.

pantheism, in which God and the universe are strictly identical. For the panentheist, God has an identity of his own, that is, he is something which the universe is not. On the other hand, the universe is part of the reality of God. It is God.[39]

Perennial Philosophy

Up until the early twentieth century, perennial philosophy, also known as perennial tradition or perennialism, had historically been a philosophical tradition that incorporated the beliefs of pre-Christian philosophers about God, man, knowledge, and virtue.[40] The philosophy was labeled "perennial" due to a belief that certain basic truths about man, knowledge, virtue, and God blossomed throughout history in all world cultures, resembling a perennial flower that blooms on a recurring basis.[41] But during the twentieth century, perennial philosophy became popularized through Aldous Huxley's book *The Perennial Philosophy*, and the term was applied to "a range of esoteric and syncretistic religious movements."[42] Huxley's perennial philosophy was different from the pre-twentieth-century classical version.

Theologian James Cutsinger differentiates the modern perennial philosophy from the classical tradition as "a broader way to refer to the idea that all of the world's great religious traditions are expressions of a single, saving truth."[43] According to Cutsinger, Huxley's perennialism endorses multiple paths to God.[44] Cutsinger states that "The [modern] perennial philosophy may be classified as a kind of pluralism," and he confirms that

> a perennialist asserts that there is one divine Source of all wisdom, which has repeatedly blossomed forth throughout history. The major religions, including Hinduism, Buddhism, Taoism, Judaism, Christianity, and Islam are different forms of that wisdom and

---

39. Davie, Grass, Holmes, McDowell, and Noble, *New Dictionary of Theology*, s.v. "Panentheism."

40. Carlson, *Words of Wisdom*, 202. Cutsinger, "Christianity and Perennial Philosophy," 912.

41. Cutsinger, "Christianity and Perennial Philosophy," 912–13.

42. Carlson, *Words of Wisdom*, 14; Huxley, *Perennial Philosophy* (2009).

43. Cutsinger, "Christianity and Perennial Philosophy," 912.

44. Carlson, *Words of Wisdom*, 153–54; Cutsinger, "Christianity and Perennial Philosophy," 912.

are sometimes referred to as paths leading to the same summit or dialects of the same language.[45]

Therefore, this book will utilize Cutsinger's characterization of Huxley's perennial philosophy and define it as: "The belief that there is one God that is common to all religions with multiple existing paths to reach that God."[46]

Theological and Enneagram Works by Rohr

Richard Rohr was born March 20, 1943, and entered the Franciscan order of the Catholic Church at the age of eighteen.[47] In 1970, he received a master's degree in theology from the University of Dayton and was ordained into the Catholic priesthood. Rohr founded the Center for Action and Contemplation (CAC) in Albuquerque, New Mexico, in 1987, where he currently serves as Academic Dean of the Living School for Action and Contemplation.[48] He was first published in the 1980s and has written numerous books and articles on theology and the use of the Enneagram as a tool in the process of personal change.[49] Rohr has championed the Enneagram's ability to facilitate an increased self-awareness among its users, which helps them discover their True Self.[50] But Rohr has not stated a role for the Holy Spirit in the Enneagram process of discovering one's True Self.[51] He has, however,

45. Cutsinger, "Christianity and Perennial Philosophy," 912.

46. Cutsinger, "Christianity and Perennial Philosophy," 912.

47. "Richard Rohr, OFM," Center for Action and Contemplation.

48. "Richard Rohr, OFM," Center for Action and Contemplation.

49. Rohr and Ebert, *Discovering*; Rohr, *Divine*; Rohr, *Universal*; Rohr, *Immortal*; Rohr and Ebert, *Christian*.

50. Rohr and Ebert, *Discovering*, 13; Rohr and Ebert, *Christian*, 4–5.

51. Rohr's view of the Holy Spirit in the process of personal change is consistent with several of the most widely recognized Roman Catholic systematic theological works. For example, Thomas P. Rausch, the T. Marie Chilton Professor of Catholic Theology at Loyola Marymount University in Los Angeles, states that "The Spirit of God or Holy Spirit, more affect than object or even subject, personifies God's creative presence" in *Systematic Theology*, 55. The term "affect," used as a noun by Rausch, is defined as "feeling or affection" in *Merriam-Webster's Collegiate Dictionary*, 21. Rausch goes on in *Systematic* to state that "the Spirit does the work of God but seems to lack a 'face'—a *prosōpon*; the Spirit is a gift, a force, but seems not to have the individual concreteness that Greek philosophy referred to by the term hypostasis" (54). Rausch also uses an impersonal pronoun for the Holy Spirit when describing His roles during creation, inspiration of prophecy, and the messianic age: "The Spirit hovers over the waters at creation (Gen 1:2)

promoted the Enneagram as a sword of the Holy Spirit, writing, "I again offer the Enneagram as another of the endlessly brandished swords of the Holy Spirit. The Enneagram, like the Spirit of truth itself, will always set you free, but first it will make you miserable!"[52] A review of Richard Rohr's written works reveals a panentheistic theology and a perennial philosophy in both his theological works and his Enneagram works.[53]

Richard Rohr has written three books that document his theology and anthropology as well as four Enneagram books that demonstrate how Rohr puts his theology and anthropology into practice. His theological books include *Immortal Diamond: Our Search for Our True Self*; *The Universal Christ: How a Forgotten Reality Can Change Everything We See, Hope For, and Believe*; and *The Divine Dance: The Trinity and Your Transformation*.[54] He has also published various theological articles on his Center for Action and Contemplation (CAC) website.[55] Rohr's theological books and articles

---

and inspires the prophets; it will rest upon the messiah (Isa 11:2; 61:1) and be poured out on all mankind in the messianic age (Ezek 36:27; Joel 3:1–2)" (54). The Roman Catholic Church's publication *Catechism of the Catholic Church* was put into effect by Pope John Paul II in 1994, first written for bishops, then priests and other catechists who have the responsibility to teach the "People of God," *Catechism of Catholic Church*, 9. *Catechism* describes the Holy Spirit's roles as interpreter of Scripture, teacher of the faith, preparer of the human heart for reception of Christ, and giver of seven gifts that belong in their fullness only to Jesus (32–34; 283–88). Even in a full chapter treatment of the Holy Spirit, *Catechism* is noticeably missing the Spirit's role in progressive sanctification, namely because there was no part for sanctification in the process of salvation (179–96). Instead of developing the Spirit's role in a process of progressive sanctification, *Catechism* states that "Spiritual progress tends toward ever more intimate union with Christ. This union is called 'mystical' because it participates in the mystery of Christ through the sacraments" (488). Also, in *Systematic Theology: Roman Catholic Perspectives*, Galvin and Fiorenza provide limited treatment of the Holy Spirit and His various roles. Galvin and Fiorenza, *Systematic Theology*. Without a section dedicated to developing a clear definition of the *Persona* and work of the Spirit, Galvin and Fiorenza vaguely acknowledge various roles for the Spirit in the church, such as the transmission of grace through the sacraments and the facilitation of penance and reconciliation (326–27, 378, 347–49). But the authors are lacking an acknowledgement and development of a clear role of the Spirit in individual sanctification.

52. Rohr and Ebert, *Christian*, xxiii.

53. Rohr, *Universal*, 43; Rohr, *Divine*, 36–38; Rohr, *Immortal*, ix, xii, xix. Rohr is careful to delineate the difference between pantheism and panentheism as well as to clarify that he is a panentheist. For articles that Rohr has written to demonstrate his commitment to a perennial philosophy, see "The Perennial Tradition"; "Interfaith Friendship"; and "Perennial Wisdom," from the Center for Action and Contemplation.

54. Rohr, *Immortal*; Rohr, *Universal*; Rohr, *Divine*.

55. Example panentheistic theological articles written by Rohr are "A Communion

will be analyzed in this book to document his theology and anthropology. An evaluation of these works exposes Rohr's panentheistic theology, which rests on his commitment to the existence of multiple incarnations as well as to his view that all of creation—including man—was already "in Christ" at creation.[56] Corollary to his panentheistic theology, Rohr articulates an anthropology in *Immortal Diamond, The Universal Christ,* and *The Divine Dance* that confirms his view that man is basically good and in need of simply discovering his good, divine True Self.[57]

Richard Rohr has written four works on the Enneagram that demonstrate the practical outworking of his theology and anthropology. In his first Enneagram book, *Discovering the Enneagram: An Ancient Tool for a New Spiritual Journey,* Rohr begins by providing a brief history of the Enneagram symbol and the nine corresponding personality types.[58] He then gives testimony of his own initial encounter and experience with the Enneagram as a means of identifying his personal gift, one big sin, and way to self-worth.[59] Rohr then dedicates a chapter to each of the nine Enneagram numbers and evaluates them in four different ways. First, Rohr provides an overview that describes general characteristics of each personality type. Then he presents the dilemma faced by each Enneagram type, which includes the root sin and avoidance mechanism associated with each type.[60] Next, Rohr provides symbols and examples for each personality type, such as animals, nations, colors, and well-known historical figures that epitomize each Enneagram number.[61] Rohr concludes every chapter of *Discovering the Enneagram* with an explanation of how each Enneagram type can achieve *conversion* and *redemption,* two terms for which he does not provide explicit definitions.[62] Throughout *Discovering the Enneagram,*

---

of Spirits," Center for Action and Contemplation; and "Nature is Ensouled," Center for Action and Contemplation. More of Richard Rohr's theological articles are located on the CAC website and can be accessed at "Articles and Media," Center for Action and Contemplation.

56. Rohr, *Universal,* 1–2, 12, 16, 20–22; Rohr, *Divine,* 36–38; Rohr, *Immortal,* 5.

57. Rohr, *Universal,* 55–68. Rohr devoted an entire chapter in *Universal* to "Original Goodness" to articulate his anthropological presupposition that man is basically good. See also, Rohr, *Divine,* 37; Rohr, *Immortal,* 12–14.

58. Rohr, *Discovering,* 3–11.

59. Rohr, *Discovering,* 11–25.

60. Rohr, *Discovering,* 31.

61. Rohr, *Discovering,* 35–177.

62. Rohr, *Discovering,* 31, 45–49, 62–65, 76–81, 95–98, 110–14, 126–30, 143–45,

Rohr clearly endorses the Enneagram as a source of ancient wisdom for personal self-discovery of the True Self.[63]

Rohr's second book on the Enneagram, *Experiencing the Enneagram*, is composed of pieces by Rohr and several contributing authors and organized into four main areas.[64] The first two sections of *Experiencing the Enneagram* summarize the Enneagram and promote it as a viable map and path for personal change.[65] Part three broaches the possibility of using the Enneagram as a means for building community in the church.[66] The fourth section of the book consists of personal testimonies of the benefits of using the Enneagram, and the book concludes with an actual Enneagram Types Test.[67] In *Experiencing the Enneagram*, Rohr continues to develop breadth in the endorsement of the Enneagram by including other authors who favor use of the symbol and typology.[68]

Rohr's third Enneagram work, *Enneagram II: Advancing Spiritual Discernment*, was based on a two-day workshop that Rohr led in which participants who represented each of the nine Enneagram types were grouped together.[69] Within each group, participants discussed the gifts and shortcomings of their respective personality types and how they related to the events of everyday life. While Rohr's prior work *Discovering* focused more on the negative or compulsive tendencies of each personality type, *Enneagram II* presents the characteristics of each Enneagram number from a more positive perspective.[70] Throughout *Enneagram II*, Rohr continues to promote the Enneagram as a tool not only to discover oneself but also to reveal a path to God.[71]

Rohr's fourth Enneagram work, *The Enneagram: A Christian Perspective*, was published in 2001 as a re-titled revision of *Discovering the*

160–61, 174–77.

63. Rohr and Ebert, *Christian*, xvii, 4–5, 48, 201, 228.

64. Rohr and Ebert, *Experiencing*.

65. Rohr and Ebert, *Experiencing*, 3–98.

66. Rohr and Ebert, *Experiencing*, 99–178. However, Rohr did not write any of the essays included in this section.

67. Rohr and Ebert, *Experiencing*, 208–40.

68. Contributing authors in *Experiencing* include Markus Becker, Hans Neidhardt, Klaus Renn, Christian Wulf, Dietrich Koller, Dirk Meine, Wolfgang Müller, Marion Küstenmacher, Liesl Scheich, and Dieter Koller.

69. Rohr, *Enneagram II*.

70. Rohr, *Enneagram II*, 135–83.

71. Rohr, *Enneagram II*, 3–56.

Enneagram. The most significant change to this work is Rohr's revised history of the Enneagram. In *The Enneagram: A Christian Perspective*, Rohr takes a more definitive stance that the Enneagram's origin has Christian roots as he connects it to the ancient desert fathers as well as to a thirteenth-century Franciscan missionary named Ramón Lull.[72] Rohr determines that Lull's use of a nine-pointed diagram to describe names and characteristics of God among the world's major religions provides the evidence necessary to deem the Enneagram as Christian in origin.[73] Aside from these new sections, *The Enneagram: A Christian Perspective* is *Discovering the Enneagram* verbatim. Rohr further emphasizes his endorsement of the Enneagram as a Christian tool, making it explicit in the book's title revision, which applies a Christian label to each of the personality typologies.

Richard Rohr is still living and actively speaking and writing, and there are no published biographies of him. One aim of this book is to demonstrate a connection between Richard Rohr's panentheistic theology and perennial philosophy and the influence of Enneagram authors Ian Cron, Suzanne Stabile, and Christopher Heuertz's in the areas of evangelical leadership development, colleges and universities, and publishing. I requested to interview Richard Rohr face-to-face or by video in order to clarify and confirm his panentheistic theology, which rests on the following presuppositions: 1) the first incarnation occurred at creation; 2) all of creation is already "in Christ" since creation. However, the Center for Action and Contemplation (CAC) denied the interview request.[74] In this book, Rohr's

---

72. Rohr and Ebert, *Christian*, 6–21.

73. Rohr and Ebert, *Christian*, 14–18. Although the nine-pointed diagrams utilized by Lull are not the same Enneagram symbol introduced later by Gurdjieff, Rohr considers Lull's diagrams as "proto-Enneagrams."

74. The email dated July 28, 2020, declining the requested interview, states, "Hi Rhenn, Thank you for taking the time to reach out to us, as well as your interest in connecting with Fr. Richard. Fr. Richard is humbled and honored that people all over the world want to connect and go deeper with his work. Even after officially retiring from full-time ministry and significantly reducing his travel, he continued to teach widely. As interest has increased, Fr. Richard is unable to meet the many requests for his time. While he has loved interacting with so many people over the years, Fr. Richard is entering into an intentionally different lifestyle in his later years which will allow him to be more contemplative. Frankly, this means he is less accessible these days. To protect Fr. Richard's foundational hermit-like existence, as well as his reduced energy and bodily strength, we ask that you please refrain from sending unsolicited letters, emails, books or manuscripts. He currently receives upwards of 20 unsolicited books *per week* and simply doesn't have the time or space to take them in. Additionally, we are not currently accepting any unsolicited requests for speaking engagements, podcast and media interviews,

theological and anthropological presuppositions will be evaluated using the works of orthodox evangelical theologians and commentators.

Works of Enneagram Authors Influenced by Rohr

Enneagram teachers and authors such as Alice Fryling and Beth McCord have referenced the works of Richard Rohr, and Fryling even secured Rohr's personal endorsement of her Enneagram book *Mirror for the Soul: A Christian Guide to the Enneagram.*[75] Beth McCord and her husband published an Enneagram book, *Becoming Us: Using the Enneagram to Create a Thriving Gospel-Centered Marriage,* and also established a business called "Your Enneagram Coach," which provides Enneagram retreats, assessments, training, and personal coaching.[76] Fryling and McCord are examples of a growing number of Enneagram authors and trainers gaining popularity among evangelicals, but neither McCord nor Fryling have direct relational lines with Richard Rohr. However, Rohr personally taught and mentored Enneagram authors Cron, Stabile, and Heuertz, and these three authors have each proven to be popular and influential among evangelicals.[77] Therefore, the Enneagram works of Cron, Stabile, and Heuertz, along with their relationships with Rohr, will be the focus of evaluating how Rohr's theological and anthropological influence has made its way into evangelicalism.

Richard Rohr was a mutual friend of Ian Cron and Suzanne Stabile, who coauthored *The Road Back to You: An Enneagram Journey of Self-Discovery,* in which they promote the Enneagram as a helpful self-awareness

book endorsements, or contributions to written works. We apologize for any inconvenience or disappointment this may have caused, but thank you for understanding. If you have any further questions or concerns, please do not hesitate to contact us. Peace and every good, Community Engagement Team Center for Action and Contemplation."

75. Fryling, *Mirror*. Richard Rohr provided a back-cover endorsement of *Mirror*. Fryling refers to Rohr several times in *Mirror* and also quotes him (9–10). Beth and Jeff McCord include Rohr's book *The Enneagram: A Christian Perspective* as a reference in their own work, *Becoming Us: Using the Enneagram to Create a Thriving Gospel-Centered Marriage.*

76. The McCords established "Your Enneagram Coach," where "Beth [McCord] is now leading the industry in simplifying the deep truths of the Enneagram from a Biblical perspective." More about the McCord's and "Your Enneagram Coach" can be accessed at "Founders of Your Enneagram Coach," Your Enneagram Coach.

77. Veinot, Veinot, and Montenegro, *Richard Rohr*, 22, 26; DeWaay, *Enneagram*, location 28.

tool for one's journey to self and to God.[78] Cron is an Episcopal clergyman and popular speaker on Christian spirituality and the Enneagram.[79] He is a trained psychotherapist and counselor who has written several best-selling books, including his autobiography.[80] He received a Dove award for co-writing the 2015 Inspirational Song of the Year, and he hosts a weekly podcast that "explores the mystery of the human personality and how we can use the Enneagram typing system as a tool to become our most authentic selves."[81] Rohr's influence on both Cron and Stabile is evident throughout *The Road Back to You* not only in their direct quotes from Rohr but also in their use of the term True Self to describe a person's good, divine identity, which the Enneagram enables them to discover.[82]

After working with Cron on *The Road Back to You*, Suzanne Stabile wrote *The Path Between Us: An Enneagram Journey to Healthy Relationships*.[83] Richard Rohr was Stabile's personal Enneagram mentor, and he is one of the people to whom she dedicates the book. She has been an instructor at Rohr's Center for Action and Contemplation (CAC) in New Mexico and also taught with Rohr internationally.[84] Suzanne Stabile is married to Reverend Joseph Stabile, a United Methodist pastor, with whom she co-founded Life in the Trinity Ministry and the Micah Center in Dallas.[85] She has led over five hundred Enneagram workshops and lectured at the Perkins School of Theology (Southern Methodist University), Brite Divinity School (Texas Christian University), Seminary of the Southwest, and

---

78. Cron and Stabile, *Road*, 17, 19.

79. InterVarsity Press author profile: "Ian Morgan Cron," InterVarsity Press.

80. Amazon author profile: "Ian Morgan Cron," Amazon.

81. Cron has featured evangelical pastors and artists on his weekly podcast. Notable proponents of the Enneagram who have participated on Cron's podcast include Richard Rohr, Chris Heuertz, Amy Grant, Carey Nieuwhof, Drew and Ellie Holcomb, Jonathan Merritt, Rob Bell, Jen Hatmaker, and Christian musical band Tenth Avenue North. "Typology," Typology Podcast.

82. Cron and Stabile, *Road*, 23–24, 31, 34, 230. The referenced uses of the term True Self by Cron and Stabile are not meant to be a complete list of all uses of the term in *Road*.

83. Stabile, *Path*.

84. InterVarsity Press author profile: "Suzanne Stabile," InterVarsity Press.

85. The Micah Center is home to Life in the Trinity Ministry, a Christian non-profit located in Dallas, Texas, that is an "inclusive ministry that uses Christian principles to encourage civility, foster personal growth, and to work toward the creation of community among all peoples." See "About LTM," Life in the Trinity Ministry.

Harvard Divinity School.[86] She is the creator and host of *The Enneagram Journey* podcast.[87]

In *The Road Back to You*, Stabile and Cron focus on applying the Enneagram to discovering one's self and *God*, but in *The Path Between Us*, Stabile champions the Enneagram's use in discovering one's self and *others*. In *The Path Between Us*, Stabile acknowledges that people view the world in different ways and benefit from a type of "translator," and she also claims that if people want to sincerely grow in their relationships with others and be personally transformed, then the Enneagram "is one of the most helpful translation tools available."[88] Consistent with that of Rohr and Cron, Stabile's Enneagram process of change presupposes the existence of a hidden True Self in every person that is good. In both her writing and personalized training, Stabile has endorsed and taught that the Enneagram is the most effective tool for discovering one's hidden, good True Self.[89]

Christopher Heuertz, a popular author, speaker, Enneagram coach, and anti-human trafficking activist, has also been heavily influenced by Richard Rohr.[90] Heuertz was raised in a Christian home and attended both Catholic and Christian private schools before studying at Asbury University in Kentucky.[91] He was mentored for three years by Mother Teresa and eventually worked with an international advocacy and development organization, Word Made Flesh, for almost twenty years, serving victims of human and sex trafficking.[92]

Heuertz's influence among younger, socially conscious Christians is significant. He is considered a forerunner in the New Friar Movement, an emerging social movement where individuals and communities "live the gospel" among the poorest communities on earth,[93] and in 2011, *Outreach*

86. See "Meet Suzanne," Life in the Trinity Ministry; and "Take Action," Life in the Trinity Ministry.

87. Stabile has hosted such notable guests as Brian McLaren, Rachel Cruz, and Luke Norsworthy. See "Podcast," The Enneagram Journey.

88. Stabile, *Path*, 2–3.

89. Cron and Stabile, *Road*, 23–24, 31, 34, 230.

90. Heuertz has written several books including *Simple Spirituality*; and Heuertz and Pohl, *Friendship at the Margins*.

91. Heuertz, *Sacred*, 29.

92. "About Me," Chris Heuertz; see "About Us," Word Made Flesh.

93. Bessenecker, *The New Friars*. In the early 2000s, InterVarsity Press and the Center for Reconciliation at Duke Divinity School formed a partnership to publish a book series called *Resources for Reconciliation*, and the stated purpose of the series was to "pursue

magazine named Heuertz among "30 Emerging Influencers Reshaping Leadership."[94] His most recent work, *The Sacred Enneagram: Finding Your Unique Path to Spiritual Growth,* is an Amazon bestseller. Heuertz dedicates *The Sacred Enneagram* to Richard Rohr and three others, and Rohr wrote the foreword for the book. Heuertz demonstrates heavy influence from Rohr in his endorsement of the Enneagram as a tool for illuminating "what's good and true and beautiful about each of us."[95] Consistent with Rohr, Cron, and Stabile, Christopher Heuertz characterizes the Enneagram as a tool that "reveals our path for recovering our true identity and helps us navigate the journey home to God."[96]

Why Rohr's Theology and Anthropology Needs Evaluation

Richard Rohr has influenced Enneagram authors who are popular among evangelicals; therefore, his theology and anthropology should be examined and compared to that of orthodox evangelical theologians in order to determine whether the Enneagram is an appropriate biblical tool for use by evangelicals. Rohr has taught a panentheism—a theology that God is *in* all of creation—that is based on the two foundational doctrines of 1) an incarnation that occurred at creation and 2) an all-inclusive interpretation of the biblical term "in Christ."[97] According to Rohr, God's act of entering into all of His creation means that all of creation—including mankind—has had a divine nature since creation.[98] Similarly, Rohr's all-inclusive interpretation

---

hope in areas of brokenness, including the family, the city, the poor, the disabled, Christianity and Islam, racial and ethnic divisions, violent conflicts, and the environment." Each book in the series "is authored by two leading voices, one in the field of practice or grassroots experience, the other from the academy." Heuertz and Pohl's *Friendship at the Margins* was a book in that series, and Christopher Heuertz was chosen by Duke and InterVarsity Press as the grassroots co-author along with Christine Pohl, Professor Emeritus at Asbury Theological Seminary, the academy representative. Heuertz has contributed in mainstream Christian and secular publications such as *Christianity Today, Relevant* magazine, and the "On Faith" section of the *Washington Post.* For more biographical information about Christopher Heuertz, his personal website can be accessed at chrisheuertz.com.

94. "Leadership," *Outreach,* 64–68.

95. Heuertz, *Sacred,* 16.

96. Heuertz, *Sacred,* 23.

97. For a more detailed definition of panentheism, see "Definition of Terms: Panentheism" on pages 7–8.

98. Rohr, *Universal,* 20–23.

of "in Christ" means that man needs only to discover his own good True Self, which has always existed.[99]

Because Rohr maintains that the first incarnation occurred at creation, an evangelical doctrine of *incarnation* will be established by surveying various theologians who are representative of orthodox evangelical theology. This book will source the systematic theological works of Herman Bavinck, Millard Erickson, John Frame, Stanley Grenz, and Wayne Grudem and document the points of consensus among these theologians on the doctrine of *incarnation*. The doctrine of *incarnation* will be evaluated specifically to determine whether biblical support exists for the first universal incarnation that Rohr promotes as well as to determine the nature of God's relationship with his creation.

The second foundational doctrine Richard Rohr uses to support his panentheism is an all-inclusive interpretation of the biblical term "in Christ."[100] Once Rohr claims the existence of a first incarnation that occurred at creation, his presupposition that all of creation is already "in Christ" closely follows. Rohr refers to specific Bible verses from the Apostle Paul's epistles to support his panentheistic notion that all of creation is already "in Christ."[101] Therefore, an examination of each of the "in Christ" passages referenced by Rohr will help determine whether Rohr's all-inclusive interpretation of "in Christ" is consistent with orthodox evangelical theology. The works of commentators Jay Adams, John MacArthur, J. B. Lightfoot, Richard Melick, and Wayne Wiersbe are considered to be representative of orthodox evangelical theology and will be consulted for each of the four passages that Rohr uses as support for his concept of "in Christ."

Richard Rohr's panentheism relies on the occurrence of a first incarnation *at* creation and an all-inclusive interpretation of the biblical term "in Christ," and Rohr's panentheism produces an anthropological presupposition that man is basically good and divine in nature. This interpretation warrants a response from the biblical anthropology of orthodox evangelical theologians. The works of orthodox evangelical theologians who have written specifically on anthropology will prove useful here. The writings of Marc Cortez, Anthony Hoekema, and Owen Strachan are considered to be

---

99. Rohr, *Immortal*, vii–26.

100. Rohr, *Universal*, 43–46.

101. The primary verses that Rohr uses to substantiate his claim that all of creation has been "in Christ" since creation are Colossians 1:19–20; Ephesians 1:3–4; Ephesians 1:9–10; and 1 Corinthians 15:28.

representative of orthodox evangelical anthropology and will be consulted specifically in the areas of man's sin nature, man's need for salvation, and the Bible as God's tool to point man to salvation in Christ alone. A brief review of these orthodox evangelical systematic theologians, commentators, and their respective works follows.

Representative Orthodox Evangelical Authors on "Incarnation"

Herman Bavinck was a nineteenth-century theologian whose four-volume *Reformed Dogmatics* is a culmination of his study of four centuries of Dutch Reformed theologians in which he "seriously engaged other theological traditions, notably the Roman Catholic and the modern liberal Protestant ones."[102] *The Wonderful Works of God* is Bavinck's compendium of his multi-volume *Reformed Dogmatics*. Bavinck wrote *The Wonderful Works of God* ten years after succeeding Abraham Kuyper as the chair of theology at The Free University of Amsterdam.[103] The sections of *The Wonderful Works of God* that most apply to an analysis of incarnation are "The Divine and Human Nature of Christ" and "Creation and Providence."[104]

Theologian Millard Erickson has served as a pastor and seminary dean at several schools, including Southwestern Baptist Theological Seminary, Western Seminary (Portland and San Jose campuses), and Baylor University.[105] In his systematic theology, *Christian Theology*, Millard Erickson addresses the concept of incarnation in several different sections. The chapters that provide the most applicable analysis of incarnation, specifically in response to Richard Rohr's use of that term, include "The Person of Christ" and "God's Originating Work: Creation."[106] Contrary to Rohr's claim that God entered into all of creation *at* creation, Erickson argues throughout *Christian Theology* that God is separate and independent from all that He has created.[107]

---

102. Bolt, "Editor's Introduction," 16–17.

103. Bavinck, *Wonderful*, xvii.

104. Bavinck, *Wonderful*, 144–65, 290–311.

105. "Authors: Millard J. Erickson," Baker Publishing Group, http://bakerpublishing-group.com/authors/millard-j-erickson/43.

106. Erickson, *Christian Theology*, 337–57, 603–74.

107. Erickson, *Christian Theology*, 272.

John Frame serves as Professor of Systematic Theology and Philosophy Emeritus at the Reformed Theological Seminary, where he teaches core courses on systematic theology, apologetics, ethics, and philosophy.[108] In *Systematic Theology: An Introduction to Christian Belief*, John Frame allocates an entire chapter to his scriptural evaluation of the Person and work of Christ.[109] After confirming both the deity and humanity of Christ, Frame addresses the incarnation.[110] Frame's approach to the incarnation focuses on his explanation of *why* and *how* it happened, but throughout his discussion he confirms that the Son of God added *only* humanity to his divine nature.[111] Throughout *Systematic Theology*, Frame offers no theological argument in support of Rohr's idea that a first incarnation occurred at creation.

Stanley J. Grenz served as the Pioneer McDonald Professor of Baptist Heritage, Theology and Ethics at Carey Theological College and at Regent College in Vancouver, British Columbia, as well as Distinguished Professor of Theology at Baylor University and Truett Seminary. In *Theology for the Community of God*, Grenz approaches the incarnation from an historical perspective and explains many of the different Christological doctrines that have been maintained throughout the history of the church.[112] In *Theology for the Community of God*, Grenz affirms the incarnation as the miraculous addition of humanity to the deity of the Son of God.

Wayne Grudem is research Professor of Theology and Biblical Studies at Phoenix Seminary, and he previously taught at Trinity Evangelical Divinity School for twenty years.[113] He has also served as the president of the Council on Biblical Manhood and Womanhood and president of the Evangelical Theological Society. In *Systematic Theology: An Introduction to Biblical Doctrine*, Wayne Grudem addresses incarnation in the chapter "The

---

108. "Dr. John M. Frame," Reformed Theological Seminary, https://rts.edu/people/dr-john-m-frame-emeritus/. The RTS website states that: "Dr. Frame's research interests include theology proper (the doctrine of God), the doctrine of scripture, ethics and epistemology (the theory of knowledge). Dr. Frame began his teaching career on the faculty of Westminster Theological Seminary in Philadelphia before serving as a founding faculty member at Westminster Seminary California for more than 20 years."

109. Frame, *Systematic Theology*, 877–922.

110. Frame, *Systematic Theology*, 883–90.

111. Frame, *Systematic Theology*, 887–90.

112. Grenz, *Theology*, 383–423.

113. "Wayne Grudem," The Gospel Coalition. Grudem has written more than one hundred academic articles and over a dozen books.

Person of Christ."[114] Grudem speaks to both the humanity of the Christ and the deity of Jesus before reviewing three "inadequate views of the Person of Christ."[115] Grudem summarizes his discussion on the Person of Christ by labeling the incarnation as the most profound of miracles and mysteries in the Bible.[116] He concludes that

> It [the incarnation] is by far the most amazing miracle of the entire Bible—far more amazing than the resurrection and more amazing even than the creation of the universe. The fact that the infinite, omnipotent, eternal Son of God could become man and join himself to a human nature forever, so that infinite God became one person with finite man, will remain for eternity the most profound miracle and the most profound mystery in all the universe.[117]

Representative Orthodox Evangelical Commentators on "in Christ"

Jay Adams was founder of the Association of Certified Biblical Counselors (ACBC, formerly NANC), the Christian Counseling and Educational Foundation (CCEF), and the Institute for Nouthetic Studies.[118] Jay Adams's commentary series *The Christian Counselor's Commentary* will be consulted for each of the "in Christ" passages that are evaluated in this book. Specifically, the series volumes titled *Galatians, Ephesians, Colossians, and Philemon* and *I & II Corinthians* will be utilized.[119] Throughout his commentary series, Adams offers a perspective that is unique to biblical counseling ministry done under the authority of Scripture in the context of the local church.

John MacArthur is the pastor-teacher of Grace Community Church in Sun Valley, California, as well as an author, conference speaker, chancellor of The Master's University and Seminary, and featured teacher with the

---

114. Grudem, *Systematic Theology*, 529–67.

115. Grudem, *Systematic Theology*, 554–56.

116. Grudem, *Systematic Theology*, 563.

117. Grudem, *Systematic Theology*, 563.

118. "Jay E. Adams," Institute for Nouthetic Studies. Adams also served as a professor at Westminster Theological Seminary in Philadelphia and as the director of the doctoral program at Westminster Theological Seminary.

119. MacArthur, *Colossians and Philemon*, 6–8.

Grace to You media ministry.[120] In his 34-volume work *The MacArthur New Testament Commentary*, he provides a "basically explanatory, or expository" evaluation of New Testament scriptural passages.[121] Throughout the series, MacArthur focuses on the major doctrines in each biblical book by exposing his readers to linguistic evaluations of the texts under consideration. But his approach throughout the series is to explain the Scriptures to his readers and help them apply those passages to their own lives. The specific volumes that will be utilized in this book are *1 Corinthians* and *Colossians and Philemon*.[122]

J. B. Lightfoot was an English theologian, preacher, and canon of St. Paul's Cathedral during the second half of the nineteenth century.[123] His writings include essays on biblical and historical subject matter, commentaries on Pauline epistles, and studies on the Apostolic Fathers. Lightfoot's commentary on Colossians will be utilized to evaluate two of the passages that Richard Rohr references in *The Universal Christ* as support for his proposition that all of creation was already "in Christ" at creation.[124] In his Colossians commentary, Lightfoot focuses mainly on the plentitude, or fullness of divine powers and attributes, of the incarnate Christ.

One volume from the *Word Biblical Commentary Series* will be utilized to evaluate passages from the book of Ephesians, and a similar volume from *The New American Commentary* series will be resourced for the Colossians passages that Richard Rohr references in his effort to support his claim that all of the universe is already "in Christ." The author of the *Word Biblical Commentary Series* commentary on Ephesians is Andrew Lincoln, and the author of *The New American Commentary* Colossians volume is Richard Melick.[125] Lincoln is Emeritus Professor of New Testament at the University of Gloucestershire, and Melick is Distinguished Senior Professor of New Testament Studies at Gateway Seminary.[126] Warren Wiersbe's *The Bible Exposition Commentary* will also be used to evaluate each of the "in

120. "About John MacArthur," Grace to You.

121. MacArthur, *Colossians and Philemon*, vi.

122. MacArthur, *1 Corinthians*; MacArthur, *Colossians and Philemon*.

123. "J. B. Lightfoot," InterVarsity Press.

124. Lightfoot, *Colossians and Philemon*; Rohr, *Universal*, 48. Rohr references Colossians 1:19–20 and Colossians 3:11 to support his claim that all of creation has been "in Christ" since the creation event.

125. Lincoln, *Ephesians*; Melick, *Philippians, Colossians, Philemon*.

126. "Truth on Trial," Wipf and Stock Publishers. "Richard R. Melick, Jr," Gateway Seminary.

Christ" passages referenced by Richard Rohr in *The Universal Christ* and *The Divine Dance.*[127]

Representative Authors
on Orthodox Evangelical Anthropology

Mark Cortez is Professor of Theology at Wheaton College and a leading expert in theological anthropology, which is "an area of theology that focuses on what Christians believe about human persons."[128] He has written multiple books on the subject, and his works *Resourcing Theological Anthropology* and *Theological Anthropology: A Guide for the Perplexed* will be utilized to evaluate man's sin nature and need for salvation.[129]

Before his death in 1988, Anthony Hoekema served as Associate Professor of Bible at Calvin College in Grand Rapids, Michigan. In *Created in God's Image*, Hoekema attempts "to set forth what the Bible teaches about the nature and destiny of human beings."[130] The most relevant chapters of Hoekema's *Created in God's Image* that will be used to critique Rohr's anthropology are "Man as a Created Person" and "The Nature of Sin."[131]

Owen Strachan is Associate Professor of Christian Theology and Director of the Center for Public Theology at Midwestern Baptist Theological Seminary.[132] Strachan has written several works on theology and anthropology, and his work *Reenchanting Humanity: A Theology of Mankind* will be resourced on the issue of man's sin nature and need for salvation. The sections of *Reenchanting Humanity* that most directly address man's sin nature and need for salvation are "Image," "Depravity," "Contingency," and "Christ."[133] These anthropological works of Cortez, Hoekema, and Strachan will be utilized to identify areas of orthodox evangelical theological consensus related to man's sin nature and man's need for salvation.

---

127. Wiersbe, *New Testament*.

128. "Marc Cortez," Wheaton College.

129. Cortez, *ReSourcing*; Cortez, *Theological Anthropology*.

130. Hoekema, *Created*, ix.

131. Hoekema, *Created*, 5–10, 168–86.

132. "Owen Strachan," Midwestern Baptist Theological Seminary.

133. Strachan, *Reenchanting Humanity*, 7–94, 313–84.

Conclusion

The nine-point Enneagram symbol was introduced to the Western world in the early 1900s by the mystic G.I. Gurdjieff. Decades later, a Gestalt psychiatrist, Claudio Naranjo, worked with a Bolivian named Oscar Ichazo during the 1960s to overlay nine Ennea-Type personality typologies onto the nine-point symbol that Gurdjieff brought to the Western world. Naranjo went on to teach the nine Ennea-Types to Catholic priests who utilized the Enneagram at seminaries and spiritual retreats during the 1970s. Father Richard Rohr, a student and eventual teacher of the Enneagram, went on to write the highly influential work *Discovering the Enneagram*. Rohr personally taught and mentored other Enneagram authors such as Ian Cron, Suzanne Stabile, and Christopher Heuertz, who have become popular among evangelical Christians.

A survey of Richard Rohr's theological and Enneagram works has exposed some concerning doctrinal positions—namely panentheism, multiple incarnations, and universalism—that warrant deeper evaluation and comparison with orthodox evangelical theology. Should Christians be troubled that Rohr's foundational Enneagram theology is panentheistic? Why does this matter? How does Rohr's panentheism inform his universalism, and how does this affect a Christian's decision to accept or reject the Enneagram? This chapter has provided an overview of representative authors and works of Enneagram theology alongside selected works of orthodox evangelical theologians and commentators that will be used to evaluate whether Rohr's Enneagram theology qualifies for prudent Christian use. We will now move into a deeper explanation and examination of Rohr's Enneagram theology and connect his panentheism to his universalism.

2

Panentheism, Multiple Incarnations, and Universal Salvation

Given Richard Rohr's influence on Enneagram authors who are popular among evangelical Christians, how does a knowledge of Rohr's theology affect evangelicals' decision to accept or reject the Enneagram? Does knowledge of Rohr's theology change an evangelical view of the Enneagram, and why is this important? An examination of the theology from which the Enneagram comes raises questions about potential dangers for evangelicals using the Enneagram.

In order to gain proper context for Richard Rohr's theological influence on various Enneagram authors popular among evangelical Christians, the reader will benefit from an understanding of the foundations of Rohr's panentheistic theology as revealed in his theological works *The Universal Christ: How a Forgotten Reality Can Change Everything We See, Hope For, and Believe*; *The Divine Dance: The Trinity and Your Transformation*; and *Immortal Diamond: The Search For Our True Self*, as well as in various theological articles he has written and posted on his Center for Action and Contemplation (CAC) website.[1] Understanding Richard Rohr's theological doctrine is important because the concepts and terms he uses in his theological works are "connected to the terms he applies to the Enneagram."[2] Rohr's panentheistic doctrine of God and man is demonstrated in his use of

1. Rohr, *Universal*; Rohr, *Divine*; Rohr, *Immortal*. Rohr's website for his Center for Action and Contemplation can be accessed at https://cac.org.

2. Veinot, Veinot, and Montenegro, *Richard Rohr*, 70.

the term True Self throughout his theological and Enneagram works, and his theological influence on Enneagram authors Cron, Stabile, and Heuertz is evident in their own extensive use of that same term.[3]

Rohr has advanced his panentheistic theology by arguing two main premises about what happened at the actual event of creation. His initial premise is that the *first* incarnation of Christ occurred at creation, and his second premise is that the biblical term "in Christ" confirms that all of creation was unified with God at creation. Both of these foundational propositions will be evaluated after an overview and demonstration of Richard Rohr's panentheism from his theological works.

Richard Rohr's Panentheism Explained

Richard Rohr has repeatedly and emphatically demonstrated his commitment to a panentheistic view of God throughout his theological writings. For example, in the dedication of his *New York Times* bestseller *The Universal Christ*, Rohr was careful not to miss an opportunity to clarify his allegiance to a panentheistic theology. He wrote, "I dedicate this book to my beloved fifteen-year-old Lab, Venus, who I had to release to God while beginning to write this book. Without any apology, lightweight theology, or fear of heresy, I can appropriately say that Venus was also Christ for me."[4] Throughout his theological works *The Universal Christ*, *The Divine Dance*, and *Immortal Diamond*, as well as many of his CAC website articles, Rohr consistently confirms that his God and his Christ dwell in all of creation, including in his own dog. Rohr even prays to Brother Sun and Sister Moon.[5] He proposes that God is a "Life Energy" that exists in and between every object and is "coterminous with the ever-larger universe we are discovering, and totally inclusive."[6] Rohr has also characterized God as "the flow who flows through everything, without exception, and who has done

---

3. Examples of Enneagram authors using the term True Self can be found in the following locations: Rohr and Ebert, *Christian*, xvii, 4–5, 48, 201, 228; Cron and Stabile, *Road*, 23–24, 31, 34, 230; Heuertz, *Sacred*, 11, 15, 22–23, 25–27, 31–32, 37, 39, 43, 53. These references to each author's use of the term True Self in their Enneagram works are not represented as their only uses of the term.

4. Rohr, *Universal*, dedication page.

5. Rohr, "The Christification of the Universe."

6. Rohr, *Divine*, 37.

so *from the beginning* [emphasis added]."[7] A corollary to Rohr's claim that God indwelled all things at creation is a presupposition that *all* things are holy because God is *in* them. Rohr has confirmed this position throughout his theological writings and even explicitly states that "Everything is holy, for those who have learned to see."[8]

The two foundational premises that Richard Rohr uses to support the panentheism that he advances in his theological works are a proposition that the "first incarnation" occurred at creation and his interpretation of the term "in Christ." Rohr maintains that at the event of the first incarnation, the infinite creator God put himself *in* all of creation *at* creation.[9] Corollary to his claim of what took place at the first incarnation of creation, Rohr also proposes that all of creation—including mankind—is therefore already "in Christ."[10]

In *The Universal Christ*, Richard Rohr proposes that an understanding of the word *Christ* is the key to reopening "that ancient door of faith," and he presents a concept of Christ that portrays an anointing of *all* creation during the events of creation described in Genesis.[11] Rohr suggests that his readers consider such provocative questions as, "What if Christ is a name for *the transcendent within* of every 'thing' in the universe?" and "What if Christ is *another name for everything*—in its fullness?"[12] Rohr encourages his readers to embrace the version of Christ that he proposes has always existed in all things, and he instructs them to do so by switching "from looking at God to looking out *from* God" who dwells in them.[13]

In his theological works, Rohr even establishes and defends his own use of the term "the Christ Mystery" as "the indwelling of the Divine Presence in everyone and everything since the beginning of time as we know it."[14] Rohr states that "God loves things by becoming them," and he appeals to Romans 8:19ff and 1 Corinthians 11:17ff to develop his term "Divine

---

7. Rohr, *Divine*, 37.

8. Rohr, *Universal*, 22. Rohr states that "The whole of creation—not just Jesus—is the beloved community, the partner in the divine dance. Everything is the 'child of God.' No exceptions." Rohr, *Divine*, 37.

9. Rohr, *Universal*, 12, 16, 20–22.

10. Rohr, *Universal*, 12, 16, 20–22.

11. Rohr, *Universal*, 5.

12. Rohr, *Universal*, 5.

13. Rohr, *Immortal*, xxiv.

14. Rohr, *Universal*, 1–2; Rohr, *Immortal*, xiii, 17, 57.

Presence."[15] Rohr claims that "Through the act of creation God manifested the eternally outflowing Divine Presence into the physical and material world. Ordinary matter is the hiding place for Spirit, and thus the very body of God."[16] Rohr and the Enneagram authors whom he influenced would go on to utilize the term Divine Presence, sometimes shortened into "Divine," to describe their panentheistic god and his presence in *all* of creation.[17]

Rohr also appeals to Colossians 3:11 to support the position that Christ is in all creation, focusing on the last words of the verse: "but Christ is all, and in all."[18] Rohr interprets Paul's words to indicate the Apostle's own understanding of what Rohr calls "the Gospel of Incarnation" that occurred at creation.[19] In both *Immortal Diamond* and *The Universal Christ*, Rohr further presses his point of Christ being in all things from creation in reference to the "Divine DNA," which he claims is found in all of creation, including man.[20] One of the major tenets of Rohr's panentheism is that all of creation's identity has *always* been in the Creator, and that all of creation will eventually gain a self-knowledge of God.[21] In *The Universal Christ*, Rohr lists the reality of this eventual self-knowledge as one of the major ramifications of the panentheism that he endorses. He states that his panentheistic view implies, therefore,

> That the Divine "DNA" of the Creator is therefore held in all the creatures. What we call the "soul" of every creature could easily be seen as *the self knowledge of God* in that creature! It knows who it is and grows into that identity, just like every seed and egg. Thus salvation might best be called "*restoration*," rather than the *retributive*

---

15. Rohr, *Universal*, 20. In Romans 8:19ff, the Apostle Paul writes about the future glory awaiting Christians and the everlasting love of God demonstrated in His sovereign choice of the elect. 1 Corinthians 11:17ff is a continuation of the Apostle Paul's instructions on orderly worship to the church in Corinth and addressess the Lord's Supper, spiritual gifts, and prophecy and tongues (1 Cor 11:17–14:40).

16. Rohr, *Universal*, 16.

17. Rohr, *Universal*, 28; Heuertz, *Sacred*, 50.

18. Rohr, *Universal*, 16.

19. Rohr, *Universal*, 16–17. Rohr claims that, "When Paul wrote, 'There is only one Christ. He is everything and he is in everything.' (Colossians 3:11); was he a naïve pantheist, or did he [Paul] really understand the full implication of the Gospel of Incarnation?" An orthodox evangelical interpretation of Colossians 3:11, along with other verses that Rohr uses to support his panentheistic theology, will be provided later in this book.

20. Rohr, *Immortal*, xiv, 17; Rohr, *Universal*, 28.

21. Rohr, *Immortal*, xiv, 17, 121; Rohr, *Universal*, 28.

agenda most of us were offered. This alone deserves to be called "divine justice."[22]

Rohr also refers to this divine DNA as an "inner destiny" and an "absolute core that knows the truth about you" and is begging to be displayed and fulfilled.[23] These direct quotes demonstrate Rohr's emphasis on the importance of people gaining self-knowledge of themselves and God since, according to Rohr, God was already in all creation from the time of the creation event itself.

Richard Rohr has not only demonstrated his commitment to a panentheistic view of his God; he has also openly criticized both Catholicism and Protestantism for their failure to recognize creation as "a cosmic event that has soaked all of history in the Divine Presence from the very beginning."[24] He has maintained that the traditional Christian view of only one incarnation is narrow, and he states, "Most Catholics and Protestants still think of the incarnation as a one-time and one-person event having to do only with the person of Jesus of Nazareth."[25] Rohr has argued that his panentheistic theology is based on God becoming one with all things at creation and refers to Genesis 1:26–27 in support of his claim that "*all* things are created in the image and likeness" of God.[26]

Don and Joy Veinot and Marcia Montenegro concur that Rohr is a panentheist, stating, "When it comes to the nature of God, Rohr openly admits to being a panentheist, and it is central to his belief system."[27] In *Enneagram: Pagan Mysticism Promoted as Christian Growth*, Bob DeWaay, founder of *Critical Issues Commentary*, agrees with Veinot and Montenegro that Richard Rohr demonstrates a commitment to panentheistic theology throughout his works and has influenced Enneagram authors Ian Cron,

22. Rohr, *Universal*, 28.

23. Rohr, *Immortal*, 17.

24. Rohr, *Universal*, 28.

25. Rohr, *Universal*, 28.

26. Rohr, *Universal*, 21. Rohr does not cite any specific Bible translation to substantiate his claim that "all things are created in the image of God." In the English Standard Version (ESV) Bible, Genesis 1:27 reads, "So God created man in his own image, in the image of God he created him; male and female he created them." In the New American Standard Bible (NASB), Genesis 1:27 reads, "God created man in his own image; in the image of God he created him; male and female he created them." Neither the ESV translation nor the NASB translation make mention of God creating *all* of creation in His image.

27. Veinot, Veinot, and Montenegro, *Richard Rohr*, 72.

Suzanne Stabile, and Christopher Heuertz.[28] DeWaay states, "Enneagram is based on a panentheistic view where God is in everything and lacks what we call in theology, 'aseity.'"[29]

In support of his panentheistic theology, Rohr has developed an explanation of how exactly creation became one with God. This point is foundational to Rohr's theology and anthropology, and Rohr has supported his notion that God is in all of creation by suggesting that multiple incarnations have in fact occurred throughout history. In *Universal Christ*, Rohr makes a distinction between the first and second incarnations, writing,

> This Infinite Primal Source somehow poured itself into finite, visible forms, creating everything from rocks to water, plants, organisms, animals, and human beings—everything that we see with our eyes. This self-disclosure of whomever you call God into physical creation was the *first Incarnation* (the general term for any enfleshment of spirit), long before the personal, second Incarnation that Christians believe happened with Jesus.[30]

Similarly, in *The Divine Dance*, Rohr makes a distinction between the first incarnation at creation and the second incarnation in Jesus, stating, "In the second person of the Trinity, we have the visible epiphany of the Unmanifest One. First in the form of creation itself—which is 'the Christ' in our shorthand—and secondly in personal form, whom we call 'Jesus.'"[31] Rohr confirms his belief that three actual incarnations have happened throughout history and claims that many well-intentioned Christians have missed the first and third incarnations.[32] He states,

> Ironically, millions of the very devout who are waiting for the "Second Coming" have largely missed the first—and the third! I'll say it again: God loves things by becoming them. And as we've

28. DeWaay, *Enneagram*, location 162 of 676.

29. DeWaay, *Enneagram*, location 162 of 676. Aseity is defined as the concept that "God is self-existent, self-sufficient and self-sustaining ('divine aseity'): God exists necessarily, with no need of help or support from the created order (cf. Acts 17:23–25). Divine aseity is God's quality of having life in and from himself. It denies any account of God which suggests he needs the world to be who he is." Davie, Grass, Holmes, McDowell, and Noble, *New Dictionary of Theology*, "The Uncommunicated Perfections," location 14354 of 37751.

30. Rohr, *Universal*, 12. For more examples of Rohr's references to multiple incarnations, see *Universal*, 13; and *Divine*, 52, 114, 145.

31. Rohr, *Divine*, 145.

32. Rohr, *Universal*, 20.

just seen, God did so in the creation of the universe and of Jesus, and continues to do so in the ongoing human Body of Christ (1 Corinthians 12:12ff), and even in simple elements like bread and wine. Sadly, we have a whole section of Christianity that is looking for—even praying for—an exit from God's ongoing creation toward some kind of Armageddon or Rapture. Talk about missing the point! The most effective lies are often the really big ones.[33]

Richard Rohr's panentheistic theology requires the existence of an historical event in which God actually entered into all of creation. If Rohr could establish an incarnational incident at which God entered into *all* of mankind, he could then build a case that all of mankind has a divine nature. By establishing the existence of man's divine nature, Rohr could then develop an anthropological presupposition that man has a hidden, good True Self that can be discovered using the Enneagram to gain self-knowledge.

Rohr's Concept of the First Incarnation at Creation

Richard Rohr attempts to undergird his panentheistic theology by declaring that the first incarnation of Christ occurred at creation.[34] He characterizes in "Franciscan language" that "creation is the First Bible, and it existed for 13.7 billion years before the second Bible was written."[35] Rohr is careful to differentiate between this first incarnation that occurred at creation and what most Christians traditionally identify as the only incarnation—the virgin birth of the God-Man, Jesus. For example, while Rohr acknowledges that the birth of Jesus is in fact the particular incarnation that "demonstrated God's radical unity with humanity," he also points out that "The incarnation, then, is not only 'God becoming Jesus.'"[36] According to Rohr, the advent of Jesus was the *second* incarnation, which was made possible by the *first* incarnation when God united himself with creation. Rohr suggests

33. Rohr, *Universal*, 20.

34. Rohr, *Universal*, 12–15; Rohr, *Immortal*, 25.

35. Rohr, *Universal*, 12. For more examples of Rohr's references to multiple incarnations see *Universal*, 13; and *Divine*, 52, 114, 145.

36. Rohr, *Divine*, 13. Throughout *The Divine Dance*, Richard Rohr claims to maintain a doctrine of the Trinity, but he differentiates between Jesus and Christ. See also *Universal*, 47, where in a discussion about the resurrection of Jesus, Rohr writes, "Most of us know about Jesus walking this [resurrection] journey, but far fewer know that Christ is the collective and eternal manifestation of the same—and that 'the Christ' image includes all of us and every thing."

that "instead of saying that God came *into* the world through Jesus, maybe it would be better to say that Jesus came *out of* an already Christ-soaked world. The second incarnation flowed out of the first, out of God's loving union with physical creation."[37]

Rohr further differentiates between Christ and Jesus, and he appeals to Scripture to substantiate this difference. He claims that "Numerous Scriptures make it very clear that this Christ existed 'from the beginning' (John 1:1–18, Colossians 1:15–20, and Ephesians 1:3–14 being primary sources), *so the Christ cannot be coterminous with Jesus.*"[38] In an effort to not be misunderstood on this point, Richard Rohr clarifies the distinction that he himself makes between his proposed universal Christ and the Christ of traditional Christianity. Rohr's Christ is an anointing of *all* creation that occurred *at* creation, and this universal Christ is not to be confused with the anointed man Jesus. Rohr argues that "by attaching the word 'Christ' to Jesus as if it were his last name, instead of a means by which God's presence has enchanted all matter throughout all of history, Christians got pretty sloppy in their thinking."[39] Also, Rohr's concept of a universal Christ requires God to enter into all of creation at creation.

Richard Rohr contends in *The Universal Christ, The Divine Dance,* and in several of his published articles that God became one with all the universe at creation. His explanation of this idea makes reference to the Bible for support, and Rohr states, "But in this book [*The Universal Christ*], I want to suggest that the first incarnation was the moment described in Genesis 1, when God joined in unity with the physical universe and became the light inside of everything."[40]

Regarding a doctrine of *Imago Dei*, Richard Rohr has denied the exclusive claim of mankind as God's ordained image bearers.[41] Instead, Rohr explains that all of universal creation was created in the image of God, stating, "For Christians, this universal pattern perfectly mimics the inner life of the Trinity in Christian theology, which is our template for how reality unfolds, since *all things* are created 'in the image and likeness' of God (Genesis 1:26–27)."[42] But the Bible translations generally accepted by evangeli-

---

37. Rohr, *Divine*, 15.

38. Rohr, *Divine*, 17.

39. Rohr, *Universal*, 17.

40. Rohr, *Universal*, 13.

41. Rohr, *Universal*, 21.

42. Rohr, *Universal*, 21.

cal Christians refer to mankind exclusively as being created in the image of God, thereby rendering Rohr's claim that all things are created in the image of God contrary to Scripture itself.[43]

We have seen that Richard Rohr's panentheism relies on the existence of an actual historical event in which God entered into all of creation and made all things—including man's good True Self—already "in Christ." It has also been demonstrated that Rohr taught that three incarnations of God—creation, Jesus, and the Body of Christ—have already taken place in history.[44] But it is Rohr's proposition that the first incarnation of God occurred at creation that most significantly affects his theology and anthropology because it provides Rohr with the historical event that his panentheistic theology requires for the Divine Presence to enter into all creation, including man. According to Rohr, it was there at the first incarnation that God put himself *into* all creation, including *into* man, and each human being's good, divine True Self came into being.[45] This leads us to an examination of the doctrine of incarnation taught by several representative orthodox evangelical systematic theologians in order to establish areas of evangelical agreement. It also provides an opportunity to contrast those points of evangelical theological consensus on incarnation with Rohr's claim that the first incarnation occurred at creation.

An Orthodox Evangelical Doctrine of Incarnation

Because Richard Rohr has embraced a notion that the first incarnation occurred at creation when God entered into all of creation, an appraisal of

43. See Genesis 1:26–27 in the New American Standard Bible (NASB); English Standard Version (ESV); Holman Christian Standard Bible (HCSB); and New International Version (NIV) translations. Translations commonly used by Roman Catholics, such as the Revised Standard Version Catholic Edition (RSVCE), New American Bible (NAB), and New Jerusalem Bible (NJB) also confirm in Genesis 1:26–27 that *only* mankind was created in the image of God.

44. Rohr maintains that three distinct incarnations have happened throughout history. In his work *The Universal Christ*, he states that "Many are still praying and waiting for something that has already been given to us three times: first in creation; second in Jesus, so that we could hear him, see him with our eyes, watch him, and touch him with our hands, the Word who is life (1 John 1–2); and third, in the ongoing beloved community (what Christians call the Body of Christ) which is still evolving throughout all of human history (Romans 8:18ff). We are still in the Flow," 20.

45. Rohr, *Divine*, vii–viii, xiii, 1–26; Rohr and Ebert, *Christian*, xvi–xvii, 4–5; Rohr, *Universal*, 25–37.

incarnation from an orthodox evangelical perspective is warranted. There-fore, this section will evaluate the writings of representative orthodox evangelical theologians on the subject of incarnation, documenting areas of common agreement.[46] The points of consensus among orthodox evan-gelical theologians on the doctrine of incarnation will now be presented.

The Incarnation Occurred Only Once

Systematic theologian Herman Bavinck describes God's speaking to man through His Son as special revelation that "stands in continuous relationship to general revelation but is at the same time essentially distinguished from it."[47] Stanley Grenz concurs with Bavinck that creation is an act of general revelation, while the incarnation of Jesus is an act of special revelation.[48] Bavinck refers to 1 John and to the Gospel of John to support his claim that Jesus was the Word become flesh as a man and is still the incarnate Word in the church now and for eternity.[49] However, Bavinck does not argue for any type of incarnation of the Word at creation, maintaining instead that through the event of the incarnation, the Father gave the Son to the world, the Son Himself descended from heaven, and the Son was conceived by the Holy Spirit.[50] Bavinck and Grenz confirm that the incarnation was limited to human flesh in the Person of the God-Man Jesus.

Bavinck points out that the entire human race benefitted from the incarnation of the Son, but he is careful not to imply that the incarnation constituted a salvific event in itself. He maintains that "In His incarnation, Christ honored the whole human race, and became a brother of all men

46. Herman Bavinck, Millard Erickson, John M. Frame, Stanley J. Grenz, and Wayne Grudem were sourced as representative orthodox evangelical theologians because their works are frequently utilized as the systematic theological texts at evangelical theological institutions. Erickson has taught at a wide range of evangelical seminaries, including Southwestern Baptist Theological Seminary, Western Seminary, and Baylor University. Frame taught at Westminster Seminary for twenty years and currently teaches theology at the Reformed Theological Seminary. Grudem taught at Trinity Evangelical Divinity School for twenty years and currently serves at Phoenix Seminary. Bavinck occupied the chair of theology at the Free University of Amsterdam University, succeeding Abraham Kuyper. Grenz served as Distinguished Professor of Theology at Baylor University and Truett Seminary.

47. Bavinck, *Wonderful*, 47.

48. Grenz, *Theology*, 396.

49. Bavinck, *Wonderful*, 96.

50. Bavinck, *Wonderful*, 134.

according to the flesh. The light shines in the darkness and by His coming into the world enlightens every man. The world was made by Him, and the fact remains so, though it did not know Him."[51] But Bavinck directly refutes any concepts that the incarnation of the Son occurred at creation or that the incarnation itself applied a universal salvation for man. In his discussion of the human nature of Christ in *The Wonderful Works of God*, Bavinck confirms that the creation of all things, along with the eternal generation of the Son, actually *made ready* the incarnation of the Son.[52] Bavinck clarifies that the incarnation event was separate from the creation event.

Bavinck also recognizes that the incarnation of the Son was part of a greater salvation plan, but that the incarnation was not salvific in and of itself. He writes,

> If we are to understand the incarnation aright, we can say that the generation of the Son and the creation of the world were preparatory to the incarnation of the Word. This is not at all to say that the generation and the creation already contain the incarnation. For Scripture always related the incarnation of the Son to the redemption from sin and the accomplishment of salvation.[53]

John Frame concurs with Bavinck on the salvific purpose of the incarnation as part of God's plan for making salvation possible for man. But like Bavinck, Frame also clarifies that the incarnation was not to be equated with salvation. He writes, "the Son of God became incarnate for a distinct purpose: to save his people from their sins. Everything in Scripture about the person of Christ has this work in view. As I indicated in Chapter 37 [of *Systematic Theology*], Jesus did not become incarnate for incarnation's sake, as if the incarnation were itself sufficient to save his people."[54] Bavinck and Frame deny any basis for equating the incarnation with salvation and offer no support for Rohr's claim that incarnation and salvation are interchangeable terms.[55]

51. Bavinck, *Wonderful*, 342.

52. Bavinck, *Wonderful*, 306. Bavinck never intimated that the Son of God was created. Bavinck's advocacy of the eternal generation of the Son was consistent with that advocated by Origen, that "The Son was eternally of the same nature as the Father but derived from him." Davie et al, *New Dictionary*, "Origen," location 23892 of 37751.

53. Bavinck, *Wonderful*, 306, 367. Bavinck also confirms that "Christ in His conception assumed the human nature, never again to lay it aside," but never implies that Christ's divine nature entered into any part of creation.

54. Frame, *Systematic*, 899.

55. Rohr, *Universal*, 27.

The Incarnation Was Exclusive to Jesus Christ

John Frame addresses the incarnation in several places in *Systematic Theology: An Introduction to Christian Belief.*[56] While making a distinction between a theophany and the incarnation of the Son of God, Frame concurs that the incarnation was the exclusive event of God permanently becoming human flesh.[57] He writes, "The incarnation of the Son of God in Jesus Christ is, of course, unique in human history. Jesus is a theophany, but much more. Only in the case of Jesus did God become flesh permanently, being conceived in the body of a woman, experiencing a human infancy and growth, increasing in wisdom and stature, subject to the sufferings of this life and to death itself."[58] Stanley Grenz's analysis of the incarnation focuses on the union of the preexistent eternal *Logos* with humanity, and he characterizes incarnation as something that the church has historically recognized as a Christological confession.[59] But consistent with Frame and Bavinck, Grenz clearly limits the incarnation to human flesh in the Person of Jesus of Nazareth. He affirms that "It [incarnation] capsulizes what we find in Jesus of Nazareth, namely, that he is the 'word'—the dynamic, revelatory word of God—in human form."[60]

Wayne Grudem's analysis of the incarnation concurs with Frame's and Bavinck's limitations of the incarnation to the human flesh of the God-Man Jesus. Grudem addresses the incarnation of Christ in "The Person of Christ" in *Systematic Theology: An Introduction to Biblical Doctrine.*[61] Grudem points out that, although the word "incarnation" does not explicitly occur in the Bible, the church has collectively used the term throughout history "to refer to the fact that Jesus was God in human flesh."[62] Grudem further clarifies that "The incarnation was the act of God the Son whereby he took to himself a human nature."[63] And consistent with Frame and Bavinck,

---

56. Frame, *Systematic*, 127, 390–93, 395, 883–90, 899.

57. Frame, *Systematic*, 390–93.

58. Frame, *Systematic*, 391, 395. Frame also confirms the permanently divine human nature of Jesus, who remains both God and man in heaven.

59. Grenz, *Theology*, 405–09.

60. Grenz, *Theology*, 405.

61. Grudem, *Systematic*, 529–67.

62. Grudem, *Systematic*, 543.

63. Grudem, *Systematic*, 543. Grudem highlights the intentional nature of the incarnation by pointing out that the "Latin word *incarnāre* means 'to make flesh,' and is derived from the prefix *in-* (which has a causative sense, 'to cause something to be

Grudem makes no attempt to substantiate a claim that God unified Himself with all of creation during the event of creation. Each of these theologians holds that the incarnation was limited to God the Son taking on human flesh only, and they make no mention of any notion that God entered into all of creation at the event of creation.

These systematic theologians affirm an orthodox evangelical view of the incarnation that is contrary to the view proposed by Rohr. They agree that the incarnation of the Son of God did not take place at creation and also that the incarnation of the Son of God does not represent a universal actualization of salvation for all men.

God Is Distinct from His Creation

In response to Richard Rohr's claim that the first incarnation occurred in all of creation *at* creation, an orthodox evangelical evaluation of incarnation must also address the relationship between God and his creation. If God did not indwell all of creation at the event of creation as Rohr has proposed, what then is God's relationship to his creation? The teachings of the orthodox evangelical theologians surveyed reveal a common agreement that God is distinct from all of his creation, including man.

Theologian Stanley Grenz dedicates an entire chapter in his work *Theology for the Community of God* to evaluate God as Creator, and he characterizes the work of God at creation as "bring[ing] into existence a universe which is other than God."[64] Wayne Grudem summarizes his interpretation of what Scripture teaches on the relationship between God and the universe. He writes, "The Bible teaches that God is distinct from his creation. He is not part of it, for he has made it and rules over it. The term often used to say that God is much greater than creation is the word *transcendent*. Very simply, this means that God is far 'above' the creation in the sense that he is greater than the creation and he is independent of it."[65] Systematic theologian Herman Bavinck demonstrates agreement with both Grenz and Grudem and refers to Psalm 90:2 as a scriptural passage that supports a clear distinction between God and his creation.[66] Bavinck states, "The thing

something') and the stem *caro, carnis-*, 'flesh.'"

64. Grenz, *Theology*, 129.

65. Grudem, *Systematic*, 267.

66. Bavinck, *Wonderful*, 148. Psalm 90:2 reads, "Before the mountains were brought forth, or ever you had formed the earth and the world, from everlasting to everlasting

that Holy Scripture is primarily on guard against is the confusion of God with His creation. God and the world are in essence distinguished from each other. They are distinguished as Creator and creature."[67] Bavinck's statement that God's essence and man's essence are different is significant because Rohr has maintained that man's essence is Divine.[68]

One of the primary Creator-creature distinctions advanced by both Millard Erickson and John Frame is the uniqueness of the Lord's specific ability to create being out of nothing. Erickson writes that "The Creator is unique: he is the only one who has brought reality into being."[69] Of God's unique ability and identity as Creator, Frame writes, "He is the God who 'calls into existence the things that do not exist' (Rom 4:17). Nobody else can do this. And so in Scripture there is a sharp distinction between Creator and creature, between the One who makes all things and the beings that he makes."[70] In a statement of further clarification aimed at eliminating any potential confusion, Frame adds that "There are two levels of being: God and the world. The two are distinct. God can never become the world, for he can never lose his status as the world's Creator. The world can never become God, because it can never undo the fact that it is created. And there is no third category."[71]

Stanley Grenz characterizes creation as God's act of entering into relationship with what He made, but Grenz is careful to clearly differentiate between the creation and the Creator.[72] Consistent with Bavinck, Frame, Grudem, and Erickson, Grenz states that "The faith community describes the fundamental relationship between God and the world by the terms 'Creator' and 'creation': God is the Creator of the universe, and the world is the creation of God."[73] Contrary to Rohr's claim that God indwelled all of creation at the event of creation, these orthodox evangelical theologians maintain that God is separate and distinct from all creation. And the differentiation that Erickson and Frame make between God and creation is in harmony with that made by Bavinck, Grudem, and Grenz.

---

you are God."

67. Bavinck, *Wonderful*, 148.

68. Rohr, *Christian*, 4.

69. Erickson, *Christian*, 343.

70. Frame, *Systematic*, 48.

71. Frame, *Systematic*, 49.

72. Grenz, *Theology*, 129.

73. Grenz, *Theology*, 129.

In contrast to Richard Rohr's proposed concept of incarnation, the orthodox evangelical theologians surveyed demonstrate agreement in three fundamental areas concerning the incarnation. First, they agree that the incarnation occurred only once in history.[74] This is contrary to Rohr's claim that three incarnations have occurred throughout history. The orthodox evangelical theologians surveyed also concur that the incarnation was an act in which God took on human flesh *only* in the God-Man Jesus.[75] This is in opposition to Rohr's claim that God entered into *all of creation* at the first incarnation. Finally, a survey of the writings of these orthodox evangelical theologians demonstrates their consensus that God is distinct from his creation.[76] This final point of agreement among these representative orthodox evangelical theologians is antithetical to Rohr's claim that God became one with creation at the event of creation.

Based on Richard Rohr's dogma that God indwelled all creation at the first of three historical incarnations, this analysis has demonstrated that Rohr teaches a panentheism contrary to orthodox evangelical theology. I will now demonstrate Rohr's contention that man's good True Self is already "in Christ" because God has already entered into all of creation.[77] This leads to an examination of how Rohr applies the term "in Christ" to justify his position that man's aim is to gain self-knowledge using the Enneagram to discover one's own good True Self. This examination will identify and evaluate Rohr's references to several "in Christ" passages in support of his all-inclusive salvation, later comparing his claims to the works of several representative orthodox evangelical commentators. Areas of agreement among these representative orthodox evangelical commentators on the meaning of "in Christ" in the passages Rohr references will set up a contrast to Rohr's interpretation of those same biblical passages.

---

74. Bavinck, *Wonderful*, 47, 96, 134, 306, 342, 367; Grenz, *Theology*, 396; Frame, *Systematic*, 899.

75. Frame, *Systematic*, 127, 390–93, 395, 883–90, 899; Grenz, *Theology*, 405–09; Grudem, *Systematic*, 529–67.

76. Bavinck, *Wonderful*, 148; Grenz, *Theology*, 129; Grudem, *Systematic*, 267; Erickson, *Christian*, 343; Frame, *Systematic*, 48–49.

77. Rohr, *Divine*, vii–viii, xiii, 1–26; Rohr and Ebert, *Christian*, xvi–xvii, 4–5; Rohr, *Universal*, 25–37.

Richard Rohr's Misapplication of "In Christ"

Richard Rohr has based his panentheism not only on the claim of the first incarnation taking place at creation, but also on his interpretation of the scriptural phrase "in Christ." While he has cited several "in Christ" scriptural passages in support of his all-inclusive interpretation of the term, Rohr does not exposit the "in Christ" passages themselves or provide readers with a context. In *The Universal Christ*, Rohr refers to the Apostle Paul's scriptural claim that "There is only Christ. He is everything and he is in everything" (Col 3:11) in order to clarify his own panentheistic stance. Rohr states that "If I were to write that today, people would call me a pantheist (the universe is God), whereas I am really a pan*en*theist (God lies within all things, but also transcends them), exactly like both Jesus and Paul."[78] Rohr also makes his own careful distinction between pantheism and the panentheism, which he advocates in the article "Christification of the Universe."[79] He states that God's anointing of the universe at creation "is not pantheism (God is everything), but pan*en*theism (God is *in* everything)."[80] In the same article, Rohr expresses agreement with fellow Franciscan sister and scientist Ilia Delio on her concept of "Christification." Rohr quotes Delio:

> Christ invests himself organically within all creation, immersing himself in things, in the heart of matter, and thus unifying the world. The universe is physically impregnated to the very core of its matter by the influence of his superhuman nature. Everything is physically "christified," gathered up by the incarnate Word as nourishment that assimilates, transforms, and divinizes.[81]

Richard Rohr claims the term "*en Cristo*," or "in Christ," as a scriptural basis for his panentheism.[82] He points out that the Apostle Paul used the term "in Christ" a total of 164 times in the New Testament and appeals to the term "in Christ" as proof that Paul was articulating a biblical understanding of a corporate salvation that occurred at the first incarnation of Christ at the creation.[83] In his own summary of Paul's use of the term "in

---

78. Rohr, *Universal*, 43.

79. Rohr, "Christification."

80. Rohr, "Christification."

81. Delio, *Unbearable Wholeness*, 79.

82. Rohr, *Universal*, 43–53.

83. Rohr, *Universal*, 43.

Christ," Rohr claims that the Apostle's words biblically affirm a panentheistic position, stating,

> *En Cristo* seems to be Paul's code word for *the gracious, participatory experience of salvation*, the path that he so urgently wanted to share with the world. Succinctly put, this identity means *humanity has never been separate from God*—unless and except by its own negative choice. All of us, without exception, are living inside of a cosmic identity, already in place, that is driving and guiding us forward. We are all *en Cristo*, willingly or unwillingly, happily or unhappily, consciously or unconsciously.[84]

Rohr interprets "in Christ" to mean that all of creation has already been included in the Christ *at* creation. He states that "humanity has never been separate from God."[85] This position of humanity and God being united at creation has strong implications for Rohr's anthropology, which results in a presupposition that man is holy. Don and Joy Veinot and Marcia Montenegro describe Rohr's view and interpretation of "in Christ" in this way: "Rohr expands the biblical teaching of the Incarnation—that Jesus is both divine and human—to include all creation with Christ representing a combination of spirit and matter as one throughout the universe. Christ is literally in everything, every animal, every human, every plant, etc."[86]

Richard Rohr adopts the label "Christification" for his own interpretation of all of creation being "in Christ," and he writes explicitly on this subject in articles posted on his CAC website.[87] For example, in "The Christification of the Universe," Rohr appeals to his readers to respect and care for all of creation, including others and ourselves—because God is *in* all of creation. Rohr maintains that *all* things were "Christified" at the creation event.[88] He again demonstrates his commitment to panentheism by alerting readers not to miss the fact that God is in everything. He writes, "From the way we treat the planet, other humans, and sometimes even ourselves, it seems we don't understand or really believe this. When

---

84. Rohr, *Universal*, 43.

85. Rohr, *Universal*, 43.

86. Veinot, Veinot, and Montenegro, *Richard Rohr*, 73.

87. Rohr makes no claim to coining the term "Christification," but he uses it frequently in his own articles and cites the term in the earlier work of Franciscan sister and scientist Ilia Delio. See Delio, *Unbearable Wholeness*, 79. Rohr's articles on "Christification" include Rohr, "Christification"; Rohr, "The Universe is the Body of God."

88. Rohr, "Christification."

you *don't* recognize that the Christ Mystery is universal, that God is present in—and is saving—all of creation, you can choose what you respect and what you disrespect, what you love and what you hate."[89]

Richard Rohr appeals to several scriptural passages to support his claim that all of creation is "in Christ," but he does so by way of reference to the passages and not by exposition of the passages. For example, in a section of *The Universal Christ* titled "En Cristo," Rohr makes the statement that "Every single creature—the teen mother nursing her child, every one of the twenty thousand species of butterflies, an immigrant living in fear, a blade of grass, you reading this book—are all 'in Christ' and chosen from the beginning (Ephesians 1:3, 9). What else could they be?"[90] Similarly, Rohr refers to Colossians 3:11, 1 Corinthians 15:28, and Colossians 1:19–20 in support of his all-inclusive interpretation of "in Christ," but he provides no exposition of the passages themselves.[91]

But is Rohr's interpretation of "in Christ" consistent with orthodox evangelical theology, and what are the ramifications of accepting his all-inclusive claim that the universe is already indwelled by God himself? Does the biblical term "in Christ" represent a universal salvation that can be discovered through a self-knowledge tool, or is the "in Christ" claim exclusive to repentant sinners who place saving faith in Jesus alone as proclaimed in the Bible?

An Orthodox Evangelical Interpretation of "In Christ"

Because Richard Rohr has interpreted the biblical term "in Christ" to represent what he refers to as a "corporate understanding of salvation," an evaluation of "in Christ" from an orthodox evangelical perspective is warranted.[92] The primary biblical passages that Rohr refers to in support of his claim are Colossians 1:19–20; Ephesians 1:3, 9–10; 1 Corinthians 15:28;

---

89. Rohr, "Christification."

90. Rohr, *Universal*, 44. Rohr does not explain the passage or provide a context, and instead follows this reference to Ephesians 1:3, 9 with the statement, "Salvation for Paul is an ontological and cosmological message (which is solid) before it ever becomes a moral or psychological one (which is always unstable). Pause and give that some serious thought, if you can."

91. Rohr, *Universal*, 47–48.

92. Rohr, *Universal*, 43.

and Colossians 3:11.[93] Therefore, these four "in Christ" passages have been reviewed using commentaries from several representative orthodox evangelical theologians, and the points of consensus among these commentators on the use of the term "in Christ" in each of these passages will now be presented and contrasted with Rohr's interpretation of "in Christ."[94] Each of the orthodox evangelical commentators surveyed agrees that the three books of the Bible from which Rohr draws scriptural support for his interpretation of "in Christ"—Ephesians, Corinthians, and Colossians—were written to churches of born-*again* believers.[95] An evaluation of these four passages will demonstrate that, contrary to Rohr's claim that a corporate all-inclusive salvation occurred at creation, the salvific claim of being "in Christ" is exclusive to the redeemed church made possible only by the work of the incarnate God-Man, Jesus.

Colossians 1:19–20

Colossians 1:19–20 is the first passage that will be evaluated for its use by Rohr to substantiate the claim that all of creation was already "in Christ."[96]

---

93. Rohr, *Universal*, 44, 47–48.

94. Jay Adams, John MacArthur, J. B. Lightfoot, Charles Hodge, F. F. Bruce, and Richard Melick were sourced as orthodox evangelical commentators because of the accessibility and popularity of their commentary works among evangelical pastors. Jay Adams is founder of the Association of Certified Biblical Counselors (ACBC, formerly NANC), Christian Counseling and Educational Foundation (CCEF), and the Institute for Nouthetic Studies, and his commentary offers a perspective that is unique to biblical counseling ministry done under the authority of Scripture in the context of the local church. John MacArthur is the pastor-teacher of Grace Community Church in Sun Valley, California, as well as an author, conference speaker, and chancellor of The Master's University and Seminary. In *The MacArthur New Testament Commentary*, he provides a "basically explanatory, or expository" evaluation of New Testament scriptural passages. J. B. Lightfoot was an English theologian, preacher, and canon of St. Paul's Cathedral during the second half of the nineteenth century. Lightfoot's Colossians commentary is particularly applicable to "in Christ" because it focuses mainly on the plentitude, or fullness of divine powers and attributes, of the incarnate Christ.

95. Adams, "Galatians, Ephesians, Colossians, Philemon," 67, 131. Adams notes that Ephesians 1:1 and Colossians 1:2 address the saints, or "set apart" ones, who have been faithful to the gospel and not succumbed to heresy. Adams makes it clear that saints "have and maintain faith in Him [Jesus] only by His mercy and grace." See also, Bruce, *Epistle to the Ephesians*, 25; Melick, *Philippians, Colossians, Philemon*, 189–90; MacArthur, *Colossians and Philemon*, 1–3; Lightfoot, *Colossians and Philemon*, 62–69.

96. Rohr, *Universal*, 48.

Although there is significant debate about the exact nature of the heresies that threatened the church in Colossae, there is widespread agreement that the Apostle Paul wrote the book of Colossians in order to combat false teaching that stood in direct opposition to the gospel originally preached in Colossae.[97] The Colossians 1:19–20 text reads, "For in him all the fullness of God was pleased to dwell, and through him to reconcile to himself all things, whether on earth or in heaven, making peace by the blood of his cross."[98]

Commentators MacArthur, Lightfoot, and Adams agree that Paul's use of the word πλήρωμα (*pleroma*) for "fullness" in verse 19 was intentional.[99] These commentators propose that Paul specifically used the word πλήρωμα (*pleroma*) because the Gnostics and other heretics at the time used the term to refer to divine powers and divine attributes that "they believed were divided among various emanations."[100] Both Lightfoot and MacArthur argue that Paul used the Gnostic term πλήρωμα (*pleroma*) or "plentitude" to affirm that all the fullness of God abides in the incarnation of Christ.[101] Regarding the Apostle Paul's use of the word πλήρωμα (*pleroma*), Lightfoot writes,

> In Him [Christ] resides the totality of the Divine powers and attributes. For this totality Gnostic teachers had a technical term, the πλήρωμα (*pleroma*) or *plentitude*. In contrast to their doctrine, [Paul] asserts and repeats the assertion, that the πλήρωμα (*pleroma*) abides absolutely and wholly in Christ as the Word of God. The entire light is concentrated in Him.[102]

John MacArthur concurs that "Paul counters that [Gnostic] false teaching by stating that all the fullness of deity is not spread out in small doses to a group of spirits, but fully dwells in Christ alone."[103]

---

97. Melick, *Philippians, Colossians, Philemon*, 161–65, 171–74; MacArthur, *Colossians and Philemon*, 6–8; Lightfoot, *Colossians and Philemon*, 37–54.

98. All quoted passages from the Bible are taken from the English Standard Version unless otherwise noted.

99. MacArthur, *Colossians and Philemon*, 52; Lightfoot, *St. Paul's Epistles*, 102.

100. MacArthur, *Colossians and Philemon*, 52; see also Lightfoot, *Colossians and Philemon*, 78.

101. MacArthur, *Colossians and Philemon*, 52; Lightfoot, *St. Paul's Epistles*, 102.

102. Lightfoot, *St. Paul's Epistles*, 102.

103. MacArthur, *Colossians and Philemon*, 52.

Richard Melick does not agree with MacArthur and Lightfoot on the matter of the Apostle Paul using the term πλήρωμα (*pleroma*) to specifically combat false Gnostic teaching at Colossae.[104] Instead, Melick argues that πλήρωμα (*pleroma*) simply expressed "totality," and that Paul used the term in verse 19 to make the larger basic point of "the full measure of deity" in Jesus *alone*.[105] Consistent with Adams, MacArthur, and Lightfoot, Melick puts a fine point on the specificity of the incarnation occurring only in the case of the God-Man Jesus. Referring to Colossians 1:19, Melick states,

> Here Paul stated that the Godhead determined that the human Jesus would be God, sharing all the properties, characteristics, and prerogatives of God himself. Of course, the movement in the incarnation was that God took flesh, not that a human was elevated to deity. The statement actually means that God was pleased to take human form in Jesus. He was not less than God, and he continues to be fully divine ("dwell" is present tense stressing an ongoing reality.)[106]

Jay Adams is more succinct and direct in his assessment of Paul's use of πλήρωμα (*pleroma*). In a clear endorsement of the exclusivity of the incarnation in the God-Man Jesus, Adams writes, "Paul identified the fullness with no one other than Jesus Christ Himself. Anyone who tries to find help in living this life outside the realm of Christ and His Word places himself in jeopardy."[107]

It is noteworthy that the latter part of verse 20 is specific about the event—the bloody crucifixion of the God-Man Jesus—that has made peace possible between God and his creation. Melick interprets Paul's use of "all things" in verse 20 to confirm that *all* of creation was tainted by sin: "The world was out of order and needed a correction. This was provided in Jesus."[108] Melick's statement highlights the fact that all of creation *was not* already "in Christ," and therefore the universe needed to be reconciled with the Creator God. In his commentary specific to Colossians 1:20, MacArthur cautions against interpreting "all things" as a type of universal salvation. He

---

104. Melick, *Philippians, Colossians, Philemon*, 191, 223–24.

105. Melick, *Philippians, Colossians, Philemon*, 224; Adams, "Galatians, Ephesians, Colossians, Philemon," 67, 139.

106. Melick, *Philippians, Colossians, Philemon*, 224.

107. Adams, "Galatians, Ephesians, Colossians, Philemon," 139.

108. Melick, *Philippians, Colossians, Philemon*, 225.

points out that an all-inclusive concept of "all things" being "in Christ" is inconsistent with the overall message of other biblical passages, writing,

> Some have imagined all things to include fallen men and fallen angels, and on that basis have argued for universalism, the ultimate salvation of everyone. By doing so they overlook a fundamental rule of interpretation, the *analogia Scriptura*. The principle teaches that no passage of Scripture, properly interpreted, will contradict any other passage. When we let Scripture interpret Scripture, it is clear that by all things Paul means all things for whom reconciliation is possible.[109]

An analysis of Colossians 1:19–20 by representative evangelical commentators demonstrates consensus on two points that are contrary to Rohr's incarnation and "in Christ" interpretations. These commentators first agree that the term πλήρωμα (*pleroma*) was used specifically by the Apostle Paul to describe the fullness of deity in the incarnation of Jesus *only*, and this consensus rules out Rohr's claim that all of creation is "in Christ." The representative commentators also agree that *all* of creation is fallen and in need of the salvation made possible *only* through the incarnate God-Man, Jesus. A survey of these evangelical commentators demonstrates that Rohr's claim that "in Christ" represents a "corporate understanding of salvation" is not supported by the Colossians 1:19–20 passage.[110]

Ephesians 1:3, 9–10

In Ephesians 1:3 Paul writes, "Blessed be the God and Father of our Lord Jesus Christ, who has blessed us *in Christ* with every spiritual blessing in the heavenly places." Jay Adams agrees with MacArthur, Frame, and Hodge that the proper context of this verse is God's covenant of "every spiritual blessing" made specifically to his church—and that this is *not* a universal promise of salvation and blessing for all of creation.[111] MacArthur and Hodge both clarify that the spiritual blessings Paul refers to are made accessible *because* those who trust Jesus are counted "in Christ."[112] Contrary to

---

109. MacArthur, *Colossians and Philemon*, 59.

110. Rohr, *Universal*, 43.

111. Adams, "Galatians, Ephesians, Colossians, Philemon," 67; MacArthur, *Colossians and Philemon*, vii, 2–3; Hodge, *Ephesians*, xx–xi.

112. MacArthur, *Ephesians*, 9–10; Hodge, *Ephesians*, 28–29. MacArthur specifically labels Jesus as the "Blessing Agent." Bruce, *Epistle to the Ephesians*, 27.

Rohr's claim of a universal salvation, these commentators offer no biblical support for any concept of all creation being "in Christ."

Ephesians 1:9–10 reads, "making known to us the mystery of his will, according to his purpose, which he set forth *in Christ* [emphasis added], as a plan for the fullness of time to unite all things in him, things in heaven and things on earth." In his commentary on Ephesians, F. F. Bruce interprets these verses as referring to God's "promise of the day when He [Jesus] will be head of a completely redeemed creation."[113] Although he notes the mystery of God's will in Christ Himself, Bruce acknowledges that verses 9 and 10 imply that all of creation is in need of redemption by the Person and work of God incarnate.[114] Hodge extensively evaluates possible meanings of "all things" in verse 10 before concluding that Paul is speaking specifically about the redemption of the elect.[115] But notwithstanding any disagreement among commentators on the exact meaning of "all things," the more salient point of creation needing redemption should not be lost. The need for creation to be reconciled, as acknowledged by Paul and confirmed by commentators Bruce, MacArthur, Adams, and Hodge, stands in direct contrast to Rohr's notion that all of creation was already "in Christ" at creation.

Similarly, in his discussion on eternal election, systematic theologian John Frame confirms that the Ephesians 1:3–14 passage describes an eternal election "in Christ" that involves redemption of the elect by the blood of Christ for the forgiveness of their sins.[116] Frame makes it clear that holiness for mankind is impossible apart from the bloody sacrifice of the incarnate Son. Throughout *Systematic Theology*, Frame makes no reference to any possibility of mankind being counted as "in Christ" at creation. Frame states that "We will see that [union with Christ] underlines all the works of God in our lives: election, calling, regeneration, faith, justification, adoption, sanctification, perseverance, and glorification. All of these blessings are 'in Christ.'"[117] Frame's statement is consistent with the evangelical commentaries cited, and Frame demonstrates that, contrary to Rohr, he does not include the act of creation as one of the "in Christ" works of God.

Therefore, an evangelical interpretation of "in Christ" does not support Richard Rohr's claim that man's True Self is already "in Christ." A survey

113. Bruce, *Epistle to the Ephesians*, 32–33.

114. Bruce, *Epistle to the Ephesians*, 32–33.

115. Hodge, *Ephesians*, 42.

116. Frame, *Systematic*, 218.

117. Frame, *Systematic*, 914.

of orthodox evangelical commentaries on Ephesians 1:3 and Ephesians 1:9–10 also confirms that man is fallen and in need of salvation through repentance and faith in the incarnate God-Man, Jesus. The consensus of evangelical commentaries on this "in Christ" passage is opposed to Rohr's proposition that man's solution is discovering one's good True Self using the Enneagram self-knowledge tool.

1 Corinthians 15:28

In common with his other epistles, the Apostle Paul addresses the letter of 1 Corinthians to a church of sanctified saints "in Christ Jesus" who were still struggling with a wide range of sinful practices within the local body of believers.[118] The context of chapter 15 is Paul's explanation of the resurrection of Christ and of those who are found in him, and the 58 verses of this chapter are the most extensive treatment of the resurrection in all of Scripture.[119] After reminding the Corinthians of the gospel that he had preached to them, as well as the hope that believers have in the resurrection of Christ, Paul writes in verse 28 that "When all things are subjected to him, then the Son himself will also be subjected to him who put all things in subjection under him, that God may be all in all." Here Paul presents a future picture of the obedient servant Jesus delivering up an eternal redeemed kingdom to the Father. Rohr cites the concluding phrase of verse 28, "that God may be all in all," as proof that Christ has always been in all of creation.[120] But according to the orthodox evangelical commentators surveyed, 1 Corinthians 15:28 refers to the redemptive work provided by God through the incarnate Jesus to restore and present an eternal kingdom to the Father.[121] Contrary to Rohr's claim of a "corporate understanding of salvation," these commentators offer no scriptural support for a universal redemption or salvation occurring at creation.[122] Instead, the commentators maintain a consistent orthodox evangelical doctrine—contrary to Rohr's proposed universal

---

118. 1 Corinthians 1:2 reads, "To the church of God that is in Corinth, to those sanctified in Christ Jesus, called to be saints together with all those who in every place call upon the name of our Lord Jesus Christ, both their Lord and ours."

119. MacArthur, *1 Corinthians*, 397; Adams, "I & II Corinthians," 93–99.

120. Rohr, *Universal*, 47–48.

121. MacArthur, *1 Corinthians*, 421; Grosheide, *Corinthians*, 369.

122. Rohr, *Universal*, 43.

salvation—that the redeemer Jesus and his role as mediator between man and God was necessary to make salvation possible for mankind.[123]

F. W. Grosheide clearly states his explanation of "that God may be all in all" as referring to a point in time when the application of the resurrection of Christ will be finished and death is destroyed.[124] Grosheide points out that

> The goal of Christ's subjection is *that God may be all in all.* There will be no opposition anymore. God's glory will then only be fully accomplished when all resistance has been frustrated by the mediatorship of Christ. Then God will be the One before all will kneel. God will be in all, i.e., with all, in the sense that he will rule them and possess them all.[125]

John MacArthur points to the incarnation of Jesus—not an incarnation that occurred at creation—as a vital component for the fulfilment of the eternal purpose of redeeming and resurrecting a kingdom to present to the Father.[126]

But the primary point of man *needing* redemption should not be lost, and an orthodox evangelical interpretation of "in Christ" is inclusive *only* of those who have been redeemed by the blood of the risen Son of God. All of mankind, as the "supreme creature of God," was tainted at the Fall along with all of creation and is in need of redemption.[127] We have seen that the scriptural picture of sinful man being separated from his Creator is in direct contrast to Rohr's proposal of mankind, along will all of creation, being "in Christ" from creation.

Colossians 3:11

In the third chapter of Colossians, the Apostle Paul reminds born-again believers that *if* they had in fact died to their old selves and been raised with Christ, they have been given the ability to put to death the old sinful practices that defined them before they were "hidden with Christ in God"

---

123. Adams, "I & II Corinthians," 96; Grosheide, *Corinthians*, 369; MacArthur, *1 Corinthians*, 416–18.

124. Grosheide, *Corinthians*, 369–70.

125. Grosheide, *Corinthians*, 370.

126. MacArthur, *1 Corinthians*, 420–21; Adams, "I & II Corinthians," 95–96.

127. MacArthur, *1 Corinthians*, 421.

(Col 3:3).[128] Paul goes on to conclude his description of "old self" practices (Col 3:5–9) by imploring believers to "put on the new self, which is being renewed in knowledge after the image of its creator" (Col 3:10). Richard Melick reinforces that these new-self values that Paul presents are rooted in each individual's conversion, which "includes a radical change of mind which produces the desire for separation from the world."[129] There is no hint of universal salvation in the passage. The context of Paul's instructions is a local body of born-again believers from diverse backgrounds, and the Apostle concludes his exhortation to put off the old self by clarifying that "Here there is not Greek and Jew, circumcised or uncircumcised, barbarian, Scythian, slave, free; but Christ is all, and in all." Richard Rohr has referenced this specific verse to support his position that all of creation has been "in Christ" from creation.[130]

J. B. Lightfoot's interpretation of the first word of verse eleven, "Here," is helpful. According to Lightfoot, "Here" means "in this regenerate life, in this spiritual region into which the believer is transferred *in Christ*," further confirming that Paul was not endorsing any type of universal salvation.[131] MacArthur and Adams concur with Lightfoot that new birth in Christ is the prerequisite for the church of redeemed believers to be able to recognize Christ's elimination of man-made social distinctions.[132]

John MacArthur and Wayne Wiersbe both propose that the theme of the entire book of Colossians can be summed up in the latter part of verse 11: "Christ is all, and in all."[133] Specific to Colossians 3:11, MacArthur confirms Paul's focus on an equal standing and value of all born-again believers—regardless of their race or social class—who are *in Christ*. MacArthur writes, "There is no place for man-made barriers in the church since Christ is all, and in all. Because Christ indwells all believers, all are equal.

---

128. Paul's qualification of those who possess the ability to put off the old self and put on the new is stated in Colossians 3:1 as being contingent on their own dying to old self and being born again in Christ. Paul's challenge to believers in Colossae to check their own salvation ("If then you have been raised in Christ") refutes any claim of a universal salvation applied at creation.

129. Melick, *Philippians, Colossians, Philemon*, 279.

130. Rohr, *Universal*, 48.

131. Lightfoot, *Colossians and Philemon*, 109.

132. MacArthur, *Colossians and Philemon*, 151; Adams, *Colossians*, 158.

133. MacArthur, *Colossians and Philemon*, 9. Wiersbe, *New Testament*, vol. 2, 137.

He breaks down all racial, religious, cultural, and social barriers, and makes believers into one new man (Eph. 2:15)."[134]

Wiersbe, MacArthur, and Lightfoot recognize that Paul's choice of four antithetical examples in verse 11 demonstrates the abolition of distinctions among those who are in Christ, and these specific examples are in "special reference to immediate circumstances of the Colossian church" for the purpose of refuting express heresies at work there.[135] Jay Adams maintains a more eternal perspective in his interpretation of verse 11 and encourages counselors to remind counselees that within the church and before God, no one person or group should have an advantage over another. But Adams adds that although some distinct advantages are clearly visible even among born-again believers in this earthly life, those distinctions will one day be non-existent in the presence of God.[136] Each of these orthodox evangelical commentators maintains that the context of *Christ being all* was in the church of redeemed believers.

Lightfoot summarizes the concept of *Christ being in all*: "Christ has dispossessed and obliterated all distinctions of religious prerogative and intellectual preeminence and social caste. Christ has submitted himself for all these."[137] MacArthur recognizes Paul's claim as distinctive for *believers* in whom Christ dwells, with no intimation of a universal salvation for all of creation. There is consensus among these orthodox evangelical commentators that in Colossians 3:11 Paul makes clear that there is no place for barriers in the church: "Because Christ indwells all believers, all are equal."[138] But again we see that the claim of being "in Christ" is exclusive to the universal church, which is made up of repentant sinners who have placed saving faith in the Person and work of the risen God-Man, Jesus.

134. MacArthur, *Colossians and Philemon*, 153.

135. Quote from Lightfoot, *Colossians and Philemon*, 109–11. Lightfoot points out that Paul's choice of "Greek and Jew" and "circumcised and uncircumcised" addresses theological and physical distinctions held by the Judaism heresy. Similarly, "barbarian and Scythian (the lowest type of barbarian)" addresses educational and intellectual differences among Gnostics. According to Lightfoot, the inclusion of "slave or free" is not meant to address a distinction necessarily unique to the Colossian church, but that a common distinction is made nonetheless. See also Wiersbe, *New Testament*, vol. 2, 137; MacArthur, *Colossians and Philemon*, 151–53.

136. Adams, *Colossians*, 158.

137. Lightfoot, *Colossians and Philemon*, 111.

138. MacArthur, *Colossians and Philemon*, 153.

It has been demonstrated that, contrary to Rohr's "corporate understanding of salvation" which he derives from several "in Christ" Bible passages, an orthodox evangelical interpretation of "in Christ" confirms that *no* universal act of salvation coincided with the act of creation.[139] In sharp contrast to the good True Self portrayed in Rohr's theological and Enneagram works, these representative evangelical commentaries reveal that man has a fallen nature and needs redemption, which is made possible *only* through the saving work of the incarnate God-Man. The consensus of orthodox evangelical Christian commentators discredits Rohr's claim that the Enneagram is a useful Christian tool for helping people discover their good True Self, and there is also no support offered from these commentators for Rohr's proposed universal salvation for all of humanity. These orthodox evangelical commentators also further clarify that the claim of being "in Christ" is reserved for repentant sinners who have placed their faith in the Person and work of the resurrected incarnate God-Man, Jesus. This exclusive evangelical Christian doctrine of being "in Christ" helps invalidate Rohr's claim that all of humanity has been "in Christ" ever since an incarnation that occurred at creation.

Conclusion

The theology from which the Enneagram comes has raised valid questions about whether evangelical Christians should use the Enneagram. Richard Rohr's theology promotes not only a universal salvation for all of creation, but also the existence of man's good True Self, and there are dangers associated with advocating the use of any type of tool built on such a faulty theological system.

In the systematic theologies of the orthodox evangelical systematic theologians surveyed, the authors offer no reference or support for more than one incarnation occurring at any time in history. They each maintain a dogma of only one incarnation, having occurred at the birth of Jesus, the God-Man. The surveyed theologians also unanimously agree that the biblical incarnation involved God the Son taking on human flesh *only* in the Person of Jesus. They offer no proposition that God became one with all of creation at the creation event. The written works of these orthodox evangelical theologians also demonstrate a clear distinction between the Creator and the creation. Each theologian confirms that God has never

139. Rohr, *Universal*, 43.

enjoined himself with his creation, and the views of these representative Orthodox evangelical theologians reject the incarnational claims made by Richard Rohr.

In the evangelical commentaries concerning the "in Christ" passages Rohr uses in support of panentheism, the writers offer no indication or support for the notion that all of creation has been "in Christ" from the time of creation. Instead, the commentators concur that mankind, along with all of creation, needs redemption and reconciliation with God, which is made possible only through the Person and work of the obedient Savior Jesus. The commentators agree that instead of the term "in Christ" representing an all-inclusive anointing of the universe at creation, the term correctly refers to the status of redeemed believers who have repented of an individual life of sin and placed saving faith in the incarnate, resurrected Son of God, Jesus. Further, the commentators agree that the concept of Christ being *in all* is not a proof text for universal salvation, but instead correctly describes Christ's elimination of social boundaries and establishment of an equality of all believers within the confines of God's redeemed community—the church.

We have seen that Richard Rohr combines an all-inclusive interpretation of the biblical term "in Christ" with his premise of a first incarnation in all of creation at creation. According to Enneagram theology, this first incarnation results in the existence of a good True Self that man needs simply to discover. But if Rohr's claim that all of mankind is already "in Christ" is faulty, what are the potential dangers to evangelicalism associated with use of the Enneagram? The following chapter will examine Richard Rohr's naturalistic anthropology, which results from his panentheistic theology, and evaluate Rohr's anthropological presupposition that man's True Self is good.

3

The Good True Self and Multiple Paths to God

Richard Rohr's panentheism promotes not only a universal salvation for all of creation, but it also argues for the existence of man's inherently good True Self that needs self-discovery, not salvation. Understanding the theology behind the Enneagram has raised legitimate concerns about whether the Enneagram is biblical and appropriate for use by evangelical Christians. But if the theological foundations of the Enneagram are faulty and inconsistent with the Bible, is it prudent to accept the Enneagram as a legitimate Christian tool? What are the implications of Christians adopting the ideology behind the term True Self from Enneagram authors, and is the underlying anthropology consistent with evangelical Christianity? Should evangelicals overlook Rohr's belief in multiple paths to God, or does Rohr's pluralism disqualify the Enneagram from being considered a Christian tool? In order to gain proper context for Richard Rohr's anthropological influence on various Enneagram authors who are popular among evangelical Christians, the reader will benefit from understanding 1) Rohr's anthropological presupposition of the goodness of man, 2) his treatment of the doctrine of original sin, and 3) his commitment to multiple paths to God.

Original Goodness, Not Original Sin

In *The Universal Christ*, Richard Rohr builds an anthropology on a foundational theology that teaches that God became all things and that God's image was therefore undeniably in *all* things.[1] According to Rohr, this image was given to all of creation equally, and he claims that there is nothing that humans could do to increase or decrease God's divine nature in them.[2] In fact, Rohr uses different labels such as "original participation," "original blessing," or "original innocence" to describe the distribution of "divine DNA" among all creatures[3]

Rohr also acknowledges that even though God indwells all of creation, it could possibly *appear* to man that he is separated from God. Rohr characterizes this problem of separation from God as something that exists in man's mind only and explicitly states of himself that "I have never been separate from God, nor can I be, except in my mind."[4] Rohr claims that the pristine universal gift of the image of God became tainted only when the concept of original sin was given birth in the mind of man. Rohr cites Augustine as the primary culprit and originator of what Rohr considers to be contaminating, extra-biblical thought:

> this picture [of the universal image of God] was complicated when the concept of original sin entered the Christian mind. In this idea—first put forth by Augustine in the fifth century, but never mentioned in the Bible—we emphasized that human beings were born into "sin" because Adam and Eve "offended God" by eating from the "tree of the knowledge of good and evil." As punishment, God cast them out of the Garden of Eden. This strange concept of

---

1. Rohr, *Universal*, 16, 20, 60–61; Rohr, *Divine*, 174–76; Rohr, *Immortal*, 60.

2. Rohr, *Universal*, 61; Rohr, *Divine*, 174–76.

3. Rohr, *Universal*, 60; Rohr, *Immortal*, xiv, 17.

4. Rohr, *Universal*, 44; Arieti, "Anti-Psychoanalytic Cultural Forces," 459–72. In his article, Arieti cites three main forces that distracted humans from developing dynamic psychology prior to Freud. The three distractive forces cited by Arieti are "the prevalence of rational thinking, the tendency to suppress emotions and sensations, and the tendency to evaluate life morally" (470). Arieti credits Augustine with prioritizing the moral evaluation of an act over the emotional or rational motivations. Similar to Richard Rohr, Arieti characterizes Augustine as a man "obsessed by a sense of sin" whose goal was to "make this world a city of God, a place free of sin—but this was an almost impossible task" (469). Unlike Rohr, Arieti does not use the term "original sin" to label Augustine's concept, but Arieti does state that Augustine "thought that the newborn baby may experience sinful pleasure at the mother's breast" (469). Similar to Rohr, Arieti claims that "Augustine's ideas spread to the whole Christian world. This obsession about sin dominated the early Middle Ages; everything was examined from a judgmental point of view. This judgmental tendency which culminated in the Middle Ages, continued in the Western world, and plays a predominant role even today" (469–70). Both Rohr and Arieti cast Augustine and the concept of original sin in a negative light.

original sin does not match the way we usually think of sin, which is normally a matter of personal responsibility and culpability.[5]

Rohr juxtaposes Augustine's negative Christian perspective of original sin and its effects on man and nature described in Genesis 3 with the positive perspective that other religions associate with the creation account in Genesis 1 and 2. According to Rohr, the difference between what he calls "original blessing," or "original participation," and original sin is simply a matter of perspective and emphasis, and he points to Augustine's doctrine of original sin as the inflection point when Christian theology began emphasizing the death of Jesus over the life of Jesus.[6] Demonstrating his disapproval of the negative view of original sin adopted by Christians, Rohr writes,

> But after Augustine, most Christian theologies shifted from the positive vision of Genesis 1 to the darker vision of Genesis 3—the so-called fall, or what I am calling the "problem." Instead of embracing God's master plan for humanity and creation—what we Franciscans still call the "Primacy of Christ"—Christians shrunk our image of both Jesus and Christ, and our "Savior" became a mere Johnny-come-lately "answer" to the problem of sin, a problem that we had largely created ourselves. That's a very limited role for Jesus. His death instead of his life was defined as saving us! This is no small point. Jesus became a mere mop-up exercise for sin, and sin management has dominated the entire religious story line and agenda to this day. This is no exaggeration.[7]

Rohr dismisses the traditional Christian views of Jesus as both a Savior who shows mercy and a judge who will punish sin in the future. He sees Savior and Judge as mutually exclusive roles, and Rohr characterizes such

5. Rohr *Universal*, 61; In his article "God With Us: Meeting Christ Within Us," Rohr reinforces for his readers that any separation from God exists in their minds, writing, "the only thing that separates you from God is *the thought* that you are separate from God!" Rohr, "God with Us."

6. Rohr, *Universal*, 61–62; Rohr and Ebert, *Christian*, 34.

7. Rohr, *Universal*, 61–62. In an article titled "Let God Be God," Rohr accuses American Christianity of fabricating a God who judges. He writes, "God created human beings in God's own image, and we've returned the compliment, so to speak, by creating God in our image. In the end, we produced what was typically a small, clannish God. In America, God looks like Uncle Sam or Santa Claus, an exacting judge, or a win/lose businessman—in each case, a white male, even though 'God created humankind in God's own image; male and female God created them' (see Genesis 1:27)." Rohr, "Let God Be God."

a God as appearing to be "whimsical and untrustworthy even to the casual observer."[8] Rohr proposes that maintaining such an unrealistic view of original sin is "a key reason why people do not so much react against the Christian story line like they used to; instead, they simply refuse to take it seriously."[9] To Rohr, the doctrine of original sin is a mental stumbling block on man's road to self-discovery of one's True Self.[10]

Richard Rohr even criticizes the anthropological teaching of Martin Luther, John Calvin, and Jonathan Edwards as being especially damaging and misleading, and in his summarized view of the historical damage done since Augustine's fifth-century introduction of the doctrine of original sin, Rohr writes,

> Yet, historically, the teaching of original sin started us off on the wrong foot—*with a no instead of a yes, with a mistrust instead of a trust.* We have spent centuries trying to solve the "problem" that we're told is at the heart of our humanity. But if you start with a problem, you tend to never get beyond that mind-set. From Augustine's theological *no* the hole only got deeper. Martin Luther portrayed humans as a "pile of manure," John Calvin instituted his now-infamous doctrine of "total depravity," and poor Jonathan Edwards famously condemned New Englanders as "sinners in the hands of an angry God." No wonder Christians are accused of having a negative anthropology![11]

Rohr labels the concept of original sin as unnecessarily negative, and he presents original sin as a type of mental hole that Christianity created, perpetuated, and imputed onto man. A better starting point, according to Rohr, is the inherent goodness of all men rooted in a "positive and generous cosmic vision" when God indwelled all of creation at the first incarnation.[12]

8. Rohr, *Universal*, 63; Rohr, "The Cosmic Christ."

9. Rohr, *Universal*, 63; Rohr and Ebert, *Christian*, 25. Rohr uses the term "sin" sparingly and apologetically in *The Enneagram: A Christian Perspective*. Regarding sin, he writes that "Anyone who discovers the power and truth of the Enneagram inevitably comes to a baffling conclusion: God makes use of our sins. (We deliberately use the word 'sin,' although we know that it sounds moralizing and judgmental to many people."

10. Rohr and Ebert, *Christian*, 4–5; Rohr, *Universal*, 51.

11. Rohr, *Universal*, 62.

12. Rohr, *Universal*, 63. In his article titled "Bigger Than Christianity," Rohr chides Christians for not embracing an indwelling of creation at the first incarnation. He contends that this would enable Christians to see Christ in everything. He writes, "Many Christians have a very limited understanding of Jesus' historical or social message, and almost no understanding of the Cosmic Christ—even though it is taught clearly in

Rohr even calls into question the sincerity of one's own love for others if that love does not originate from a presupposition of man's inherent goodness. For example, he writes, "I have never met a truly compassionate or loving human being who did not have a foundational and even deep trust in the inherent goodness of human nature."[13] But is Rohr's presupposition that man is good consistent with orthodox evangelical anthropology? And should his rejection of original sin as an orthodox evangelical doctrine disqualify the Enneagram from being considered Christian?

Original Sin and Man's Depraved Nature Are Real

In *ReSourcing Theological Anthropology*, Marc Cortez emphasizes that a Christological anthropology, or understanding of who Christ is as a man, is central to understanding what it means to be human and live in the midst of a broken world.[14] Even throughout his lengthy and controversial discussion of whether the incarnate Christ had a fallen or unfallen nature, Cortez consistently confirms the reality that mankind has a sinful nature.[15] Cortez includes the sinful nature of man as a fundamental premise of his thesis that Jesus is the model of what it means to be human *in the midst of a fallen world*.[16] Similarly, in *Created in God's Image*, Anthony Hoekema states that an essential aspect of a Christian doctrine of man is a consideration of the question of original sin.[17] Hoekema defines original sin as "the sinful state and condition in which every human being is born" and differentiates it from actual sin, which he defines as "the sins of act, word, or thought that humans commit."[18] In *Reenchanting Humanity*, Owen Strachan's acknowledgment and treatment of original sin harmonizes with that of Cortez and Hoekema, and he confirms the historical reality of the fall of mankind into

---

Scripture (see John 1, Colossians 1, Ephesians 1, 1 John 1, Hebrews 1:1). Christ is often taught at the very beginning of Paul's and other New Testament authors' writings, yet we still missed it. But you can't see what you were never told to look for. Once you do see the shape and meaning of this cosmic mystery of Divine Incarnation, you'll be able to see that the Presence is everywhere." Rohr, "Bigger Than Christianity."

13. Rohr, *Universal*, 63.

14. Cortez, *ReSourcing*, 253, 259.

15. Cortez, *ReSourcing*, 130–66.

16. Cortez, *ReSourcing*, 22, 36, 169, 253, 259–60.

17. Hoekema, *Created*, 143.

18. Hoekema, *Created*, 143.

sin.[19] Strachan maintains that man has a guilt problem—not a knowledge problem—associated with his sin, and he leaves no room for a mental-only characterization of original sin. Regarding the reality of original sin and man's guilty stance before God, he writes that

> Adam's sin left him condemned before his Creator. By his sin, he dies judicially. He has no way to remove this sentence. He has forensically sinned against the Lord and disobeyed divine teaching. He is not vaguely broken; he is legally guilty, and he cannot do otherwise. Guilt in biblical terms is not a psychological sensation that a pharmacist or therapist can erase.[20]

Hoekema offers a slightly different perspective and distinguishes two aspects of original sin—guilt and pollution—defining original pollution as "the corruption of our nature that is the result of sin and produces sin."[21] He further differentiates between pervasive depravity and spiritual inability.[22] Hoekema prefers the term *pervasive depravity* to total depravity because he believes that the term *total depravity* is often misunderstood to be overly negative.[23] Hoekema characterizes human beings as pervasively depraved, which means that "(1) the corruption of original sin extends to every aspect of human nature; to one's reason and will as well as to one's appetites and impulses; and (2) there is not present in man by nature love to God as the motivating principle of his life."[24] Strachan concurs with Hoekema that "The overarching term for man's spiritual condition is this: *total depravity*."[25] Strachan also agrees with both Cortez and Hoekema that, consistent with "historic Protestant formulation of biblical teaching, sin reaches into every aspect of the human person."[26] Hoekema refers to

19. Strachan, *Reenchanting*, 78–79.

20. Strachan, *Reenchanting*, 78.

21. Hoekema, *Created*, 149–50; Frame, *Systematic*, 899.

22. Hoekema, *Created*, 150; Strachan, *Reenchanting*, 87.

23. Hoekema, *Created*, 150. Hoekema acknowledges that total depravity has been misunderstood to mean "(1) that every human being is as thoroughly depraved as he or she can possibly become; (2) that unregenerate people do not have a conscience by means of which they can distinguish between good and evil; (3) that unregenerate people will invariably indulge in every conceivable form of sin, or (4) that unregenerate people are unable to perform certain actions that are good and helpful in the sight of others." Hoekema points out that God's common grace restrains sin in unregenerate people.

24. Hoekema, *Created*, 150.

25. Strachan, *Reenchanting*, 86; Hoekema, *Created*, 150.

26. Strachan, *Reenchanting*, 86. Consistent with Hoekema's clarification of a

John 3:3 as scriptural support for his characterization of pervasive depravity, writing,

> this doctrine [of pervasive depravity] underlies all of New Testament teaching. Jesus' insistence that unless one is born again he cannot see the kingdom of God (John 3:3) implies that human beings are unable, in their natural, unregenerate state, even to see the kingdom of God, let alone enter it. The entire New Testament message is addressed to sinners who do not love God by nature, who do not love one another, and who need to be radically changed by the Holy Spirit before they will be able to do what is pleasing in God's sight.[27]

Strachan's characterization of man's situation in the context of a twenty-first century culture is antithetical to the naturalistic anthropology demonstrated in the Enneagram works of Rohr and the Enneagram authors he has influenced. In describing both man's intrinsic value and fallen nature, Strachan writes,

> Our optimistic, sin-eliding age might encourage us to fundamentally affirm ourselves as good and beautiful and perfect, but the Bible communicates the opposite. We are inestimably valuable as those made by God, but in Adam we have plunged into death and sin and evil. We cannot come to God; we cannot of ourselves know the Lord. We cannot please the Lord. We neither want nor follow God's will. In our fallenness, we can't even understand the things of God. We are totally depraved and thus totally unable to come to God.[28]

But Strachan and Hoekema assist their readers in understanding that while knowledge is not a means in itself to salvation, man's self-knowledge of his own sinful nature helps him recognize how fallen he really is.[29] This

---

misunderstood definition of "total depravity," Strachan explains that "We have corrupt natures and are guilty of sin due to Adam's fall. Evil has reached into every corner of our beings, and we are pervasively corrupted as a result. Our minds, hearts, souls, bodies, and entire beings are oriented toward wickedness; we are not as bad as we could be, left without any moral intuition or instinct whatsoever, but we are totally ruined by sin, and as such are comprehensively evil."

27. Hoekema, *Created*, 150.

28. Strachan, *Reenchanting*, 87.

29. Strachan, *Reenchanting*, 94; Hoekema, *Created*, 102–11. In chapter 6 of *Created in God's Image*, Hoekema gives a thorough treatment of "The Question of Self-Image."

biblical self-knowledge drives man back to the Lord, from whom his help and his worth come.[30]

Each of these orthodox evangelical theologians affirms that the singular problem before humanity is sin, and that the one hope for sinful humanity is the Person and work of the resurrected, incarnate God-Man Jesus.[31] The claims of these theologians contradict Rohr's unorthodox anthropology, which claims man's problem is one of mistaken identity and that man's hope is located in his ability to gain self-knowledge of his good True Self. But does Rohr demonstrate an anthropological presupposition that man is basically good in his theological works only, or is his anthropology displayed in his Enneagram works as well as the works of the Enneagram authors he influenced? Should evangelical Christians remain neutral to Rohr's anthropology, and how does his anthropology affect evangelicals' decision to accept or reject the Enneagram? We now turn our attention to how Rohr, Cron, Stabile, and Heuertz treat the concept of original sin and how they utilize the term True Self in their Enneagram works to demonstrate a commitment to an anthropological presupposition that man is basically good. This analysis will show that one cannot affirm Rohr, Cron, Stabile, and Heuertz's concept of the good True Self as described in their Enneagram works without adopting an anthropology that man is basically good and without original sin, as well as affirming that Christ's work was not necessary in order to free man from the bondage of his depraved nature.

The Enneagram Is the Tool for Self-Knowledge of the Good True Self

Man's problem, according to Richard Rohr and Enneagram authors Cron, Stabile, and Heuertz, is that man does not know who he really is; he has not yet discovered his good True Self.[32] Rohr identifies the discovery of the True Self as the knowledge-based solution to man's identity problem, and

---

30. Hoekema, *Created*, 105–06. Regarding a biblical knowledge of one's self, Hoekema states that "One must indeed first realize the magnitude of his sins against God (and this will certainly bring with it a nonflattering self-image) before he will feel the need of repenting of his sin and turning to Christ in faith." See also Strachan, *Reenchanting*, 94.

31. Strachan, *Reenchanting*, 94; Hoekema, *Created*, 133–67; Cortez, *ReSourcing*, 68–69, 78–79.

32. Examples of these Enneagram authors referring to the term True Self as the objective of self-knowledge can be found in the following locations: Rohr and Ebert, *Christian*, xvii, 4–5, 48, 201, 228; Cron and Stabile, *Road*, 23–24, 31, 34, 230; Heuertz, *Sacred*, 11, 15, 22–23, 25–27, 31–32, 37, 39, 43, 53.

he generalizes that "The true and essential work of all religion is to help us recognize and recover the divine image in everything. It is to mirror things correctly, deeply, and fully *until all things know who they are.*"[33] According to Rohr, knowledge of self is the key to finding and accepting one's good True Self, and he states that "Faith at its essential core is accepting that you are accepted."[34]

Rohr appeals to 1 John 1:21, which states that "It is not because you do not know the truth that I write to you, but because *you know it already* [emphasis added]," to support his claim that *knowledge* is the key to accessing the divine nature that resides in all of creation.[35] Rohr conflates the terms "consciousness," "soul," "the Law written in your heart (Jer 31:33)," and the "Indwelling Holy Spirit" and claims that "these terms are largely interchangeable, approaching the same theme from different backgrounds and expectations."[36] Although the epistle of 1 John is addressed to born-again believers, Rohr's interpretation of 1 John 1:21 is that "He [John] is talking about *an implanted knowing* in each of us—an inner mirror, if you will," that connects God "equally to all creatures."[37] According to Rohr, this implanted divine nature of the True Self is waiting to be discovered through self-knowledge facilitated by the Enneagram.

Richard Rohr's anthropological influence on Enneagram authors Ian Cron, Suzanne Stabile, and Christopher Heuertz is evident primarily in their use of the term True Self, which presupposes an inherent connection with the Divine. Rohr and Heuertz choose to capitalize True Self and its interchangeable terms throughout their Enneagram works, while Cron

33. Rohr, *Universal*, 59; Rohr, *Immortal*, 96.

34. Rohr, *Universal*, 29; Rohr also wrote a three-part series of articles in which he promotes the use of the Enneagram as the best tool for those wanting to increase self-knowledge and discover their True Self. Rohr, "Tool for Significant Self-Knowledge."

35. Rohr, *Universal*, 60; Rohr and Ebert, *Christian*, xi, 28–29.

36. Rohr, *Universal*, 60. In an article on the indwelling of the Holy Spirit, Rohr demonstrates his doctrine of the Holy Spirit indwelling *everyone*. He writes, "The paradox is that this True Self is immortal and indestructible, and yet it must also be awakened and chosen. The Holy Spirit is totally given and given equally to all, but it must be consciously received. The Presence needs to be recognized, honored, and drawn upon to become a Living Presence." Rohr, "Naturally Indwelling."

37. Rohr, *Universal*, 60. Rohr also uses the term "uncreated grace" and writes in *Immortal* that "The divine indwelling was a total gratuitous gift, standing presence, and guarantee; it is the Holy Spirit living within us, sometimes called the 'uncreated grace.'" Rohr, *Immortal*, 121.

and Stabile do not capitalize such terms.[38] Christian apologist and author Bob DeWaay concurs that the True Self is a key term used throughout the Enneagram works of Rohr, Cron, Stabile, and Heuertz that assumes people have an existing unfallen version of themselves that can be discovered, along with God.[39] DeWaay states that "This theme of the true self and one's true identity is certainly central to the Enneagram. These teachers [Rohr, Cron, Stabile, and Heuertz] believe that the Enneagram is a 'sacred' tool for finding one's way from the false self to the pristine, inner 'True Self' and in so doing finding the way to God."[40] DeWaay interprets Rohr, Cron, Stabile, and Heuertz's use of the term True Self as a demonstration of their belief that man has a divine nature that, according to Rohr's anthropology, was gained at creation and is waiting to be discovered.

Cron and Stabile Confirm Rohr's Anthropology

Ian Cron and Suzanne Stabile use Rohr's term True Self frequently through-out *The Road Back to You*, and they consistently demonstrate an agreement with Rohr's presupposition that man's True Self has always been connected to God since creation and must be re-discovered.[41] Cron and Stabile use the terms *true self*, *authentic self*, and *true nature* interchangeably throughout *The Road Back to You*, and the authors use each of these various terms in the context of discovering a person's original, good self, which was created in unity with God but is now hidden in their personality, or false self.[42] They first demonstrate their embrace of Rohr's panentheism and its associated term True Self (also *authentic self*) in *The Road Back to You* during a discus-sion on the "mask of personality" as a protective mechanism that covers "parts of our *authentic self*."[43] They contend that the strategies developed

38. Rohr and Ebert, *Christian*, xvii, 4–5, 48, 201, 228; Cron and Stabile, *Road*, 23–24, 31, 34, 230; Heuertz, *Sacred*, 11, 15, 22–23, 25–27, 31–32, 37, 39, 43, 53, 248; Heuertz, *Enneagram of Belonging*, 16, 19, 25.

39. DeWaay, *Enneagram*, location 217.

40. DeWaay, *Enneagram*, location 217.

41. Cron and Stabile, *Road*, 23–24, 31, 34, 230; Rohr and Ebert, *Christian*, xvii, 4–5, 48, 201, 228.

42. Cron and Stabile, *Road*, 22–23.

43. Cron and Stabile, *Road*, 22. Richard Rohr and Christopher Heuertz choose to capitalize "True Self" in their Enneagram works. Ian Cron and Suzanne Stabile choose not to capitalize "true self" in their Enneagram works. In this book, the author capitalizes True Self and the terms used interchangeably with true self based on the direct context or

during childhood become more complicated later in life so much so that "we can't tell where they end and our *true natures* begin."[44] Two sentences later, in an explanation of personality and the confusion it creates in humans, they state that each person's mask reflects "our tendency to confuse the masks we wear with our *true selves*, even long after the threats of early childhood have passed."[45] The underlying premise of Cron and Stabile's use of these interchangeable terms in these contexts is that man's true self is divine in nature and origin. And consistent with Rohr's anthropology, Cron and Stabile maintain that man needs to discover his good True Self. In a warning to the readers of *The Road Back to You* against over-identifying with the masks of their personalities, the authors demonstrate a concurrence with Rohr's anthropology in the following reminder:

> Worst of all, by overidentifying who we are with our personality we forget or lose touch with our *authentic self*—the beautiful essence of who we are. As Frederick Buechner so poignantly describes it, "The original, shimmering self gets buried so deep that most of us end up hardly living out of it at all. Instead we live out all the other selves, which we are constantly putting on and taking off like coats and hats against the world's weather."[46]

According to Cron and Stabile, there is an "original, shimmering self" that is separated not only from oneself, but also from creation. In his description of an awareness of his own personal separation from creation, as well as an underlying better version of himself yet to be fully revealed, Ian Cron states,

> Though I'm a trained counselor, I don't know exactly how, when or why this occurs, only that this idea of having lost connection with my true self rings true with my experience. How many times while spying my children play or while gazing up at the moon in a reflective moment have I felt a strange nostalgia for something or someone I lost touch with long ago? Buried in the deepest precincts of being I sense there's a truer, more luminous expression of

---

quotation of the Enneagram author he references.

44. Cron and Stabile, *Road*, 23; Rohr and Ebert, *Christian*, 25–26. Rohr characterizes a false self-image that develops in people past their childhood up until they reach the age range of 30 to 40 years old. See also Heuertz, *Sacred*, 57.

45. Cron and Stabile, *Road*, 23; Heuertz, *Sacred*, 107, 110. In *Sacred*, Heuertz refers to the "childhood wound" as something the Enneagram exposes.

46. Buechner, *Telling Secrets*. Quoted by Cron and Stabile, *Road*, 23, without a corresponding page location.

myself, and that as long as I remain estranged from it I will never feel fully alive or whole. Maybe you have felt the same.[47]

Cron maintains that he, like the rest of mankind and creation, is separated from his True Self, and that this True Self is a truer, better expression of himself.

In their attempt to connect this original True Self to creation, Cron and Stabile remind their readers of their own original good natures and affirm Rohr's knowledge-based solution, stating, "The good news is we have a God who would know our scrawny butt anywhere. He remembers who we are, the person he knit together in our mother's womb, and he wants to help restore us to our *authentic selves.*"[48] In their conclusion to *The Road Back to You*, titled "So Now What?," Cron and Stabile provide two examples of their agreement with Rohr's presupposition of man's good True Self in a review of how readers should proceed forward on their paths to self-discovery of the True Self.[49] First, they quote Catholic monk and theologian Thomas Merton's confirmation that one's need to discover his True Self is indeed man's problem in life. Merton writes, "For me to be a saint means to be myself. Therefore, *the problem of sanctity and salvation is in fact the problem of finding out who I am and of discovering my True Self.*"[50]

Further, Cron and Stabile conclude *The Road Back to You* with John O'Donohue's "Blessing for Solitude," which Cron's spiritual director had prayed over him as a blessing years before Cron himself set off on his own "journey of self-discovery and self-knowledge."[51] The prayer displays Cron and Stabile's support of Rohr's panentheistic theological presupposition that all of creation, including man, has always been connected to God and the rest of the universe. Their concluding prayer for readers emphasizes a restoration of their authentic selves to the God and universe with which

47. Cron and Stabile, *Road*, 23; Rohr and Ebert, *Christian*, 29. Rohr, Cron, Stabile, and Heuertz all have a common background of being raised in a Christian environment. Rohr maintains that "those of us who have grown up in a religious environment will find it usually takes a while before we can hear these positive voices" so that we can "discover what in us is *really* good," Rohr, *Christian*, 29.

48. Cron and Stabile, *Road*, 23.

49. Finley, *Merton's Palace of Nowhere*, 8. Thomas Merton wrote over fifty works during the 1940s–60s and is considered by many Catholics as "an excellent guide in our search for God." Cron and Stabile, *Road*, 226–30.

50. Cron and Stabile, *Road*, 230.

51. O'Donohue, "For Solitude." Quoted by Cron and Stabile, *Road*, 230, without a corresponding page location.

they are one: "May you recognize in your life the presence, power, and light of your soul. May you realize that you are never alone, that your soul in its brightness and belonging connects you intimately with the rhythm of the universe."[52]

Ian Cron and Suzanne Stabile are not the only individuals who utilize Rohr's concept of the good True Self in their Enneagram works. In *The Sacred Enneagram*, Christopher Heuertz employs the term True Self in a manner consistent with Rohr's use of the term in order to articulate the good True Self as the eventual objective of gaining self-knowledge through the Enneagram.[53]

Heuertz Confirms Rohr's Anthropology

Similarly to Cron and Stabile, Christopher Heuertz confirms Richard Rohr's anthropology through extended use of the term True Self throughout his Enneagram books. In *The Sacred Enneagram*, Heuertz titles the first chapter "The Question of Identity: Exploring Who We Are, How We Got Lost, and How We Might Find Our Way Back Home to Our True Identity."[54] In that opening chapter, Heuertz clearly demonstrates a view that man's primary problem is one of a mistaken identity, and he places much emphasis on discovering the goodness and beauty of a person's True Self. For example, Heuertz shares a story from a blind Jesuit priest at Creighton University and draws an analogy in order to demonstrate a kind of blindness that all humans have toward their good True Selves. He affirms that "When it comes to recognizing the truth of our own identities, most of us experience a symbolic version of blindness that keeps us from seeing ourselves for who we really are."[55] Heuertz introduces the term True Self in a discussion of man's pursuit of happiness and characterizes the work of Thomas Keating, a Trappist monk, in the area of contemplative practice as helping to provide a "framework for understanding the process of breaking free into our True Self."[56]

---

52. Cron and Stabile, *Road*, 230.

53. Heuertz, *Sacred*, 11, 15, 22–23, 25–27, 31–32, 37, 39, 43, 53, 248; Rohr and Ebert, *Christian*, xvii, 4–5, 48, 201, 228.

54. Heuertz, *Sacred*, 15.

55. Heuertz, *Sacred*, 16.

56. Heuertz, *Sacred*, 22; Heuertz, *Belonging*, 177–78. Along with Richard Rohr, Thomas Keating was a founding member of Christopher Heuertz's non-profit, Gravity.

In "Appendix 1: EnneaGlossary" of *The Sacred Enneagram*, Heuertz provides his own definition of True Self.[57] He defines True Self as "The integrated authentic self. Who each person is created and called to be when the heart is centered and the mind is at peace. One's essence or Essential Self."[58] In his definition of True Self, Heuertz includes several interchangeable terms such as *authentic self, essence,* and *Essential Self,* and he also demonstrates Rohr's theological influence by referring to the True Self as something that was both established at creation and divine in nature (noted by the capitalization of True Self and Essential Self).[59] Consistent with Rohr's claim that all men have a good True Self, Heuertz maintains that the Enneagram exposes the inherent holiness and divine nature of man:

> Another approach to understanding the nine types involves the exploration of the purest features of each [Enneagram] type—the Enneagram's Holy Ideas and Virtues. Much like a precious jewel, with each twist and turn reflecting the elegance of a different facet, the Enneagram also has affirmative renderings that draw attention to what is particularly beautiful about each type.[60]

Throughout *The Sacred Enneagram* and *The Enneagram of Belonging,* Heuertz consistently refers to the Enneagram as the "sacred map for our souls; a map that, when understood, leads us home to our true identity in God."[61]

Heuertz closes out the first chapter of *Sacred* by asking three prompting questions about the state of man's mistaken identity before proposing the Enneagram as the "Sacred Map" to self-knowledge.[62] He encourages

---

57. Heuertz, *Sacred,* 245–48.

58. Heuertz, *Sacred,* 248. Also, in the EnneaGlossary, Heuertz defines the False Self as "The functioning pseudo-self that perpetuates self-destructive patterns, behaviors, and tendencies based on its addictions to power and control, affection and esteem, or security and survival." Consistent with Rohr, Cron, and Stabile, Christopher Heuertz maintains that the False Self stands in our way along this path of self-discovering our True Self. Because an evaluation of the term False Self is not required to demonstrate the panentheism and anthropological presuppositions embraced and demonstrated by Enneagram authors Richard Rohr, Ian Cron, Suzanne Stabile, and Christopher Heuertz, an evaluation of the term False Self is not included in this book.

59. For example, Heuertz utilizes a capitalized version of Essence that he equates with the True Self in *Belonging,* 16, 19, 25.

60. Heuertz, *Sacred,* 35.

61. Heuertz, *Sacred,* 26; Heuertz, *Belonging,* 58; Rohr and Ebert, *Discovering,* 32, 35; Cron and Stabile, *Road,* 23–24.

62. Heuertz, *Sacred,* 29; Cron and Stabile, *Road,* 31, 34; Rohr and Ebert, *Discovering,*

his readers to ask themselves, "So how have we gotten so far off track? How do we heal ourselves from the false identities we've reinforced? Ultimately, how do we find our way home to the God of love and our true identity? This is where the Enneagram comes in. It reveals our path for recovering our true identity and helps us navigate the journey home to God."[63] Then, consistent with Rohr, Cron, and Stabile, he introduces and promotes the Enneagram as the most helpful self-knowledge tool for people to use in their journey of self-discovery.[64]

In the second chapter of *The Sacred Enneagram*, "What Is the Enneagram?: Learning the Essentials of This Ancient Tool," Christopher Heuertz demonstrates a full adoption of the term True Self and uses the term extensively to describe the eventual destination that every human being unknowingly desires to reach. After differentiating the "Enneagram of Personality" from other historical versions of the symbol, Heuertz affirms that "The contemporary Enneagram of Personality illustrates the nine ways we get lost, but also the nine ways we can come home to our True Self."[65] In a section of *The Sacred Enneagram* titled "Original Virtue = True Self or Our Essential Nature," Heuertz denies the doctrine of original sin and refers to a time in our lives when a sin-free version of us existed.[66] In touting the effectiveness of the Enneagram in discovering one's good True Self, he claims, "On the Enneagram we can map where we've come from, the departure from our essence, that original innocence we experienced in the early days of our infancy when the world actually might have seemed okay."[67]

Heuertz defines the objective of using the Enneagram as finding your True Self, and he proposes the film *The Wizard of Oz* as a narrative that portrays the journey "home to our true identity and to God."[68] According to Heuertz, we all, like Dorothy, are looking for ways to get back to our True Self. Heuertz, consistent with Rohr, maintains that an *illusion* of who we think we are stands in the way of doing the inner work required for

---

xi.

63. Heuertz, *Sacred*, 23.

64. Rohr and Ebert, *Christian*, xvi–xvii, xx, xxiii, 4–5, 32, 45; Cron and Stabile, *Road*, 10–11, 17, 19–20, 24, 31, 343–36; Heuertz, *Sacred*, 16, 23, 24–64.

65. Heuertz, *Sacred*, 25.

66. Heuertz, *Sacred*, 109; Rohr and Ebert, *Christian*, 4–5. Heuertz characterizes the Enneagram as "nine ways we can find our way back to God" on the website of his nonprofit, Gravity. Heuertz, "What Is the Enneagram?"

67. Heuertz, *Sacred*, 109.

68. Heuertz, *Sacred*, 26.

discovering one's good True Self. In his EnneaGlossary, Heuertz defines inner work as "The practice of integrating self-awareness into action toward personal growth. These efforts are largely supported by contemplative practices."[69] In *The Sacred Enneagram*, Heuertz emphasizes the need to know one's own good True Self, and, consistent with Rohr, Cron, and Stabile, he promotes the Enneagram as the most effective tool for self-discovery.[70]

It has been demonstrated that contrary to an orthodox evangelical anthropology that teaches the reality of original sin and man's fallen nature, Richard Rohr and Enneagram authors Ian Cron, Suzanne Stabile, and Christopher Heuertz promote an anthropology that acknowledges man's good True Self, which has existed since the first incarnation. These authors characterize people's problem as mistaken identity, which can be resolved by discovering who they have always been since creation, and each author promotes the Enneagram as the best tool for discovering one's True Self. But are there other concerns that Christians should have about Richard Rohr and his promotion of the Enneagram as a self-discovery tool for discovering one's True Self and God?

Rohr's Perennialism

Up until the early twentieth century, the philosophical tradition of classical perennialism had historically been labeled "perennial" due to a belief that certain basic truths about man, knowledge, virtue, and God blossomed throughout history in all world cultures on a recurring basis.[71] But a modern version of perennial philosophy, popularized by Aldous Huxley's 1945 book *The Perennial Philosophy*, is a form of pluralism teaching that all the major religions—including Hinduism, Buddhism, Taoism, Judaism, Christianity, and Islam—are different forms of a divine wisdom that lead to the same God.[72] This new perennialism represents a shift from acknowledging common themes that have been contemplated throughout human history to affirming the existence of multiple paths to God.

---

69. Heuertz, *Sacred*, 247; Rohr, "Contemplative Consciousness."

70. Heuertz, *Sacred*, 16, 23, 24–64; Rohr and Ebert, *Christian*, xvi–xvii, xx, xxiii, 4–5, 32, 45; Cron and Stabile, *Road*, 10–11, 17, 19–20, 24, 31, 343–36.

71. Carlson, *Words of Wisdom*, 202; Cutsinger, "Christianity," 912.

72. Huxley, *Perennial Philosophy*; Cutsinger, "Christianity," 912; Keene, "Perennial Philosophy," 116.

Richard Rohr adopts Huxley's perennialism and references or quotes from Huxley's work *The Perennial Philosophy* in his own articles, which promote the perennial tradition.[73] In a 2017 article titled "The Perennial Tradition: Interfaith Friendship," Rohr endorses Huxley's characterization of the perennial tradition:

> Just what is this perennial tradition? I like British philosopher Aldous Huxley's (1894–1963) description as the combination of a spiritual metaphysics, a recurring psychology of the human person, and an ethic or morality that flows from these: 1) A metaphysic which recognizes a divine Reality substantial to the world of things and lives and minds; 2) A psychology that finds in the soul something similar to, or even identical with, divine Reality; 3) An ethic that places man's [sic] final end in the knowledge of the immanent and transcendent Ground of all being.
>
> [This perennial tradition] is immemorial and universal. Rudiments of the Perennial Philosophy may be found among the traditionary lore of primitive peoples in every region of the world, and in its fully developed forms it has a place in every one of the higher religions.[74]

In another of Rohr's articles on perennialism, he agrees with a belief that all world religions are seeking the same God, and he quotes the editor of *World Wisdom Bible*, Ravi Shapiro, who characterizes God as the "Source": "Everything you see, think, feel, and imagine is part of and never apart from the same Source. We call this Source by such names as God, Reality, Brahman, Allah, One, Krishna, the Absolute, and the Nondual. The list of names is long; the reality to which they all point is the same."[75] Richard Rohr has also demonstrated an urgency to acknowledge and endorse the perennial tradition in his writing, stating, "We are rediscovering the *philosophia perennis*, shared universal truth, and at a rather quick pace—God seems urgent at this point in our tragic history."[76] Rohr is committed to teaching

---

73. Rohr, "Interfaith Friendship"; Richard Rohr, "Perennial Wisdom."

74. Rohr, "Interfaith Friendship." In the article, Rohr quotes Aldous Huxley from *The Perennial Philosophy* (1945), vii. He repeats his quotation of Huxley verbatim in a later article, "Perennial Wisdom."

75. Rohr, "Perennial Tradition," August 4, 2018. Rohr quotes Shapiro, *Perennial*; and Shapiro, *World Wisdom Bible*.

76. Rohr, "Perennial Tradition," August 17, 2019.

perennial philosophy at his Center for Action and Contemplation and has incorporated the subject into the curriculum at his Living School.[77]

The perennial philosophy of Rohr and Huxley, which endorses multiple paths to the same God, also rejects any one religion's exclusive claim to knowing the sole path to God.[78] In a 1948 book review of Huxley's *The Perennial Tradition*, James Calvin Keene, Professor of Religion at Howard University, wrote,

> As a whole the book attacks the claim of any religion to be absolute, and so will be unacceptable to Christian fundamentalist and neo-orthodox alike. It attempts to find a universal approach to religion which would regard any particular formulation as giving possibly one path leading to truth, but not as the only path.[79]

According to both Huxley and Rohr, no one religion has the right to make an exclusive claim regarding salvation.[80] Rohr has been outspoken in his rejection of Christianity's exclusive claim of salvation through faith in Jesus alone, and he has consistently attacked the specific claims of Christianity about special revelation and the need for a personal relationship with God through Christ alone.[81] In his description of the "truth" of a universal God present in all creation, Rohr reinforces his rejection of special revelation. He writes, "This [universal Christ] is good and universal truth, and does not depend on any group owning an exclusive 'divine' revelation."[82] According to Rohr, each person has no intrinsic need for salvation and instead needs only to recognize who he has always been "in Christ." Therefore, Rohr considers it arrogant for any one particular religion to make an exclusive claim to understanding *the* way of salvation for man.[83] In defense

77. Learning the perennial tradition is now part of Rohr's Living School for Action and Contemplation two-year program curriculum. He outlines the perennial tradition component of the program in "Perennial Tradition."

78. Rohr, *Universal*, 25–27, 45, 67; Huxley, *Perennial*, 200–11.

79. Keene, "Perennial Philosophy," 116.

80. Rohr, *Universal*, 27, 45; Huxley, *Perennial*, 207, 210–11.

81. For various examples of Rohr's criticisms of Christianity's claim of salvation only through a personal relationship with Jesus Christ, see Rohr, *Universal*, 20, 26–27, 45. Similarly, chapter 13 of Huxley's *The Perennial Philosophy*, titled "Salvation, Deliverance, Enlightenment," is devoted to examining areas of commonality of salvation beliefs of such world religions as Buddhism, Hinduism, and Christianity. See Huxley, *Perennial*, 200–11.

82. Rohr, *Universal*, 26.

83. Rohr, *Universal*, 48–49; Huxley, *Perennial*, 207.

of his perennialist position, he states that "Christianity has become clannish, to put it mildly. But it need not remain there."[84] Rohr has sought to eliminate what he describes as the tribal nature of Christianity by combining a concept of God that is both personal and universal. He claims that "The Christ Mystery anoints all physical matter with eternal purpose from the beginning."[85]

Rohr's perennial view of God fits well with his panentheism because it provides considerable latitude for people to believe that whatever god they choose is included in the "Primal Source" of creation. Rohr states,

> Most of the perennial traditions have offered explanations [for the creator], and they usually go something like this: Everything that exists in material form is the offspring of some Primal Source, which originally existed only as Spirit. This Infinite Primal Source somehow poured itself into finite, visible forms, creating everything from rocks to water, plants, organisms, animals, and human beings—everything we see with our eyes.[86]

In another example of his activism against Christians' exclusive claim of the special revelation of God and his Word, which is *not* available to mankind universally, Rohr claims,

> the message in this book [*The Universal Christ*] can transform the way you see and the way you live in your everyday world. It can offer you the deep and universal meaning that Western civilization seems to lack and long for today. It has the potential to re-ground Christianity as a natural religion and not one simply based on a special revelation, available only to a few lucky enlightened people.[87]

Rohr displays an intent to re-establish Christianity as a natural religion that includes everyone and everything. As an answer to Christianity's claim of salvation through Jesus Christ alone, Rohr proposes an alternate

---

84. Rohr, *Universal*, 21.

85. Rohr, *Immortal*, 17, 57; Rohr, *Universal*, 20.

86. Rohr, *Universal*, 12. In *Immortal*, Rohr demonstrates how panentheism fits well with an all-inclusive "Perennial Tradition of religion" through his interpretation of the universal term "You are that" as meaning "that the True Self, in its original, pure, primordial state, is wholly or partially identifiable *or even identical with God*, the Ultimate Reality that is the ground and origin of all phenomena." Rohr, *Immortal*, 99.

87. Rohr, *Universal*, 6.

existence of a cosmic Christ who is all-inclusive. This idea of a universal Christ, he writes,

> competes with and excludes no one, but includes everyone and everything (Acts 10:15, 34) and allows Jesus Christ to finally be a God figure worthy of the entire universe. In this understanding of the Christian message, the Creator's love and presence are grounded in the created world, and the mental distinction between "natural" and "supernatural" sort of falls apart.[88]

In another criticism of evangelicalism's claim for the need of an individual relationship with God through Christ alone, Rohr has claimed that present-day man has the ability to adopt a larger, more accurate view of exactly who his universal god really is. He claims that unless God connected man with the universe, he really was not God. Rohr states,

> Given our present evolution of consciousness, and especially the historical and technological access we now have to the "whole picture," I now wonder if a sincere person can even have a healthy and holy "personal" relationship with God if that God does not also connect them to the universal. A personal God cannot mean a smaller God, nor can God make you in any way smaller—or such would not be God.[89]

Rohr combines his perennial philosophy with his panentheism and imputes them both onto Catholicism and Protestantism by linking Christian maturity itself to one's ability to recognize that God is in everything. According to Rohr, "A mature Christian sees Christ in everything and everyone else. That is a definition that will never fail you, always demand more of you, and give you no reasons to fight, exclude, or reject anyone."[90] He eventually takes this concept beyond a simple mark of Christian maturity and defines one's ability to see the universal Christ as the criterion for

---

88. Rohr, *Universal*, 7. In "Universal Salvation: The Cosmic Christ Week 2," Rohr criticizes the concept of an individualized salvation and writes that "A universal notion of Christ takes mysticism beyond the mere individual and private level that has been seen as mysticism's weakness. If authentic God experience overcomes the primary false split between yourself and the divine, then it should also overcome the equally false split between yourself and the rest of creation." Rohr, "Universal Salvation."

89. Rohr, *Universal*, 20. Also, in *Immortal*, Rohr criticizes Protestantism as a whole for not moving "towards any notion of real or universal participation [with other world religions]" but claims that many individuals are in fact moving from Protestantism to a more universal religion. Rohr, *Immortal*, 111.

90. Rohr, *Universal*, 33.

authentic Christianity. Rohr claims, "The proof that you are a Christian is that you can see Christ everywhere else."[91] Richard Rohr has maintained an offensive posture toward evangelical Christianity and frequently criticizes the concept of a personal relationship with God through Christ alone as a divisive and clannish claim that is too small of a concept for his universal Christ.[92]

Rohr's Enneagram Works Demonstrate Multiple Paths to God

Richard Rohr also demonstrates his commitment to perennial philosophy throughout his Enneagram works. For example, in *The Enneagram: A Christian Perspective*, Rohr makes an analogy between the Enneagram and Geoffrey Chaucer's use of "at least one specific virtue as an antidote to every deadly sin" in *The Canterbury Tales*.[93] In drawing this parallel with Chaucer, Rohr goes on to state that "God would like all people to be saved, but there are many ways to the heavenly city."[94] Rohr further develops a variation of perennialism's multiple paths to God and labels the Enneagram the face of God.[95] He states, "The whole Enneagram diagram is called the 'face of God.' If you could look out at reality from nine pairs of eyes and honor all of them, you would look at reality through the eyes of God."[96] In his section of *The Enneagram: A Christian Perspective*, titled "Jesus and the Enneagram," Rohr seeks "to demonstrate to what extent each of the nine types of the Enneagram may be securely connected to Jesus Christ,"[97] and he provides an Enneagram diagram with a picture of Jesus at the center that connects Jesus to each of the nine personality types.[98] Rohr's perennial philosophical influence on Ian Cron, Suzanne Stabile, and Christopher

91. Rohr, *Universal*, 51; In *Immortal*, Rohr claims that religious people who "pick a few moral positions to give themselves a sense of worthiness and discipline" and "don't have time for the mystics" are most likely "outsiders to the very [Christ] mystery." Rohr, *Immortal*, 110.

92. Rohr, *Universal*, 26–27, 34, 45, 61–63, 66; Rohr, *Immortal*, ix, 34, 39–40, 49–55, 68–69.

93. Rohr and Ebert, *Christian*, 35.

94. Rohr and Ebert, *Christian*, 35.

95. Rohr, "Enneagram (Part 1)"; Rohr, *Christian*, 5.

96. Rohr, "Enneagram (Part 1)."

97. Rohr and Ebert, *Christian*, 233.

98. Rohr and Ebert, *Christian*, 232–46. The Enneagram diagram with Jesus at the center is Figure 20, located on page 245.

Heuertz reveals itself through the nine "paths to God" concept advocated by each of those three authors in their respective Enneagram works.

In *The Road Back to You*, Ian Cron and Suzanne Stabile demonstrate Rohr's perennial influence and endorsement of nine paths to God. For example, in a warning to their readers about using the Enneagram as a weapon against others, they affirm the Enneagram's purpose of connecting people to God in different ways and on different paths. They warn, "*The Enneagram should only be used to build others up and help them advance on their journey toward wholeness and God. Period.* We hope you take this to heart."[99] In *The Enneagram: A Christian Perspective*, Richard Rohr refers to the Enneagram as "the face of God," and in a 2019 interview with *Christian Coaching Magazine*, Suzanne Stabile confirms her adoption of Rohr's term "the face of God" to describe multiple paths to God.[100] She states that "in Christian context, the Enneagram is referred to as 'the face of God.' And, I think that's because it is representative of all of the fullness of the nine ways of seeing the world."[101]

Heuertz demonstrates an advocacy of the Enneagram as a tool that exposes nine paths back to the True Self and to God, and this exposes a perennial philosophical commitment to the concept of multiple paths to God. In the second chapter of *Sacred*, Heuertz explains to his readers that the Enneagram makes clear the nine ways to finding our way back to our True Self and to God. He states, "The contemporary Enneagram of Personality illustrates the nine ways we get lost, but also the nine ways we can come home to our True Self. Put another way, it exposes nine ways we lie to ourselves about who we think we are, nine ways we can come clean about those illusions, and nine ways we can find our way back to God."[102] Heuertz dilutes the sinful aspects of the false self, even more so than Merton and Rohr, and proposes it as something people must "come to terms with and own."[103] In *The Sacred Enneagram*, Christopher Heuertz also affirms Russ Hudson's explicit statement that an "[Enneagram] Type isn't a 'type' of person, but a path to God."[104] But does the claim of multiple

---

99. Cron and Stabile, *Road*, 38.

100. Rohr and Ebert, *Christian*, 40; Cheuk, "Path Between Us," 5:40.

101. Cheuk, "Path Between Us," 5:40.

102. Heuertz, *Sacred*, 25; Rohr and Ebert, *Christian*, 40.

103. Heuertz, *Sacred*, 58.

104. Heuertz, *Sacred*, 49. Russ Hudson was a contemporary of Richard Rohr and wrote *Personality Types: Using the Enneagram for Self-Discovery* and *The Wisdom of the*

existing paths to God disqualify the Enneagram from being considered a legitimate Christian tool?

The Biblical Claim of Salvation through Christ Alone

Richard Rohr's perennial claim of multiple paths to God is contrary to the exclusive claims of the Bible regarding the salvation of man. Scripture has recorded that Jesus of Nazareth, God incarnate, made this exclusive claim in John 14:6: "I am the way, and the truth, and the life. No one comes to the Father except through me." And the first Christ followers confirmed Jesus's exclusive claim to be the one way unto salvation for man. When the Sanhedrin in Jerusalem asked the apostle Peter to give an account for the source and name by which he had performed miracles, the apostle was clear in attributing them singularly to "the name of Jesus Christ of Nazareth."[105] Peter continued and clarified that Jesus is man's only source of salvation, proclaiming, "there is salvation in no one else, for there is no other name under heaven given among men by which we must be saved." These are two of numerous examples of how the Bible itself records the clear statements of the apostles Peter and Paul, and Jesus of Nazareth himself, testifying that there is one way to salvation, only through the God-Man Jesus.[106]

Systematic theologians who are representative of orthodox evangelical theology agree that the incarnate Son of God, Jesus of Nazareth, is the only way for man to be reconciled unto God.[107] There is no biblical support for a universal salvation or multiple paths to God. Theologian Stanley Grenz directly addresses the exclusivity of Jesus's claim to be the one way to

---

Enneagram: The Complete Guide to Psychological and Spiritual Growth for the Nine Personality Types.

105. The Sanhedrin's questions and Peter's full answer are contained in Acts 4:5–12.

106. There are other Bible passages that substantiate the exclusive claim of salvation through Christ alone. For example, 1 Timothy 2:5–6 states, "For there is one God, and there is one mediator between God and men, the man Christ Jesus, who gave himself as a ransom for all which is the testimony given at the proper time." Other supporting scriptural passages include John 10:9; Romans 10:9; John 3:36; John 3:16; John 3:18; Romans 6:23; John 8:58; and 1 John 5:20.

107. Bavinck, *Wonderful*, 138, 257, 351, 389; Frame, *Systematic*, 426, 684, 957–58, 962; Grudem, *Systematic*, 117; Erickson, *Christian*, 139–40 (footnote 35), 295, 705, 711, 1004, 1021, 1026; Grenz, *Theology*, 93, 337, 367, 450, 460, 533, 559, 570, 640, 753, 833. For background on each of these systematic theologians and why they are considered to be representative of orthodox evangelical theology, see prior footnote 47 in chapter 2.

salvation, and he cites the resurrection itself as God's definitive confirmation of Jesus's unique claim. Grenz writes,

> Taken by itself, Jesus' claim to be the unique human would have been audacious. We could view his declaration "I am the way and the truth and the life" (John 14:6) as vain and prideful. For this reason, Jesus' self-consciousness as the teacher of the truth concerning the way to life, just as his parallel claim to enjoy a special relation to the Father, called for a response from God. God must either confirm the opinion of his opponents who considered him a great sinner or acknowledge that Jesus is in truth the embodiment of true humanity. God's response came in the resurrection. By raising Jesus from the dead, God declared that this man is indeed the paradigmatic human he claimed to be.[108]

Contrary to Richard Rohr's claim that only discovery of one's good True Self is necessary for salvation, orthodox evangelical Christianity has maintained the necessity of a personal relationship with Jesus for salvation. Theologian John Frame summarizes a consensus held by Christians throughout history that has stressed the centrality and personhood of the God-Man, Jesus, as the only Savior available to man:

> So Christians of all times and places have professed that Christ himself is the center of our preaching, our gospel, our theology. "Christianity is Christ." This phrase is a way of saying that what is most important about Christian faith is not a set of doctrines or laws or practices or liturgies, but a person. To be a Christian is to have a personal relationship to Jesus Christ, in which he is our Lord and Savior.[109]

In *Reenchanting Humanity*, Strachan reminds readers that the spiritually dead must be regenerated by the work of the God-Man Jesus, and Strachan connects the work of the Word of God to the process of man's reconciliation to God. Strachan writes,

> But doctrine, the teaching of God's Word, is the only pathway to meaningful unity. Christ alone joins once-hostile people in organic, even mystical, union. Through faith and repentance, we are Christ's own body. He loves us. He will not abandon us. He shed

---

108. Grenz, *Theology*, 367.

109. Frame, *Systematic*, 877.

his blood and consented to the breaking of this body, and he gave up his spirit for us.[110]

John Frame succinctly summarizes an evangelical theological consensus that refutes Rohr's panentheism and anthropological presupposition that man is basically good. Frame writes,

> Our plight is not that we are finite, that we are not-God; and the remedy for our plight is not some new metaphysical connection to God. Rather, our plight is ethical: We have sinned, and therefore we are in a state of personal estrangement from our Creator. Jesus' incarnation was a means of bringing about reconciliation between ourselves and God.[111]

An orthodox evangelical anthropology teaches that man's need for salvation can be met only through a personal relationship with the God-Man Jesus.

Richard Rohr's theological claim that God indwelled all creation at creation has now been exposed as conflicting with Scripture and an orthodox evangelical theology. Similarly, his anthropological presupposition of man's good nature and his claim that multiple paths exist to God are both demonstrably contrary to the Bible and orthodox evangelicalism. So, the reader is now presented with the question of whether *any* theological or anthropological claim made by Richard Rohr can be trusted and labeled as "Christian." Further, can readers who claim faithfulness to orthodox evangelical theology reconcile their own personal use of anything championed by Rohr and labeled as Christian, such as the Enneagram, that has such heretical theological foundations? If the reader finds himself defending Rohr and the Enneagram writers whom Rohr has influenced, that reader must question the biblical basis for such a defense.

Conclusion

Richard Rohr's anthropological presupposition of man's inherently good nature has raised concerns about whether evangelical Christians should use the Enneagram. The reader has seen that while Richard Rohr dismisses the idea of original sin as a burdensome mental construct instituted by Augustine in the fifth century, an orthodox evangelical theology maintains

110. Strachan, *Reenchanting*, 377.
111. Frame, *Systematic*, 899.

the reality of man's depraved nature and original sin as necessary components of a biblical anthropology. This chapter provided several examples of how Enneagram authors Cron, Stabile, and Heuertz adopt Rohr's True Self term as the target of people's individual journey to self-discovery. But given the differences between Rohr's anthropology and an orthodox evangelical anthropology, the reader must now consider whether it is prudent to label or adopt the Enneagram as a Christian tool. Does the underlying theology associated with the Enneagram disqualify it from use by evangelicals?

This chapter has also established that Richard Rohr is committed to a perennial philosophy that endorses multiple paths to God, and Rohr has also championed the Enneagram as the multi-path tool for self-discovery. And although Rohr has argued against any exclusive claim of how salvation is made possible for man, an orthodox evangelical theology upholds the exclusive claim in the Bible of Jesus as the one way of salvation for sinful mankind. Rohr's contention of *multiple* ways to God contrasts with evangelical Christianity's claim of Jesus as the *only* way to God. Richard Rohr's anthropology promotes not only a good nature for man, but also the existence of multiple paths to God, and there are dangers associated with advocating the use of any type of tool built on such a faulty anthropological system.

But if Rohr holds to a defective claim that mankind's nature is inherently good, or if his allegation that multiple paths exist to God is antithetical to the claims of the Bible, what are the potential dangers to evangelicalism associated with adopting the Enneagram as a Christian tool? We will now examine Richard Rohr's relationships with Enneagram authors whom he trained and mentored, following the respective lines of influence of Ian Cron, Suzanne Stabile, and Christopher Heuertz into the areas of Christian leadership development, Christian educational institutions, and evangelical publishing. This will help the reader to better understand how and why the Enneagram has gained popularity among evangelicals.

4

The Influence of Enneagram Authors on Evangelicalism

Should an understanding of Richard Rohr's panentheistic theology and anthropology impact evangelical Christians' decision about whether to use the Enneagram? Which of Richard Rohr's relationships have served as channels for cultivating a desire among evangelical Christians to discover one's True Self through the Enneagram? In which key areas of influence have the Enneagram authors personally trained by Richard Rohr most affected evangelicalism?

In order to gain proper context for how Richard Rohr's panentheistic theology and anthropology have infiltrated evangelicalism through the Enneagram, the reader will benefit from a brief description of the origins of Rohr's connections with three specific Enneagram authors who are popular among evangelical Christians. Although Rohr's relationships with Enneagram authors Ian Cron, Suzanne Stabile, and Christopher Heuertz developed in different ways, Rohr impressed upon each of them the importance of using the Enneagram as a Christian tool for discovering one's True Self.[1] By tracing the history of Richard Rohr's personal relationships with these three Enneagram authors and their own associations with evangelical leaders and institutions, the reader will better understand how Rohr's

1. Cron and Stabile, *Road*, 11–20; Heuertz, *Sacred*, 25–51; Rohr and Ebert, *Christian*, 4–21. Bob DeWaay characterizes Richard Rohr as "the key proponent of the Enneagram, as he is praised and cited by the other authors [Cron, Stabile, and Heuertz]," DeWaay, *Enneagram*, location 42.

theological and anthropological emphasis on self-discovery of the good True Self through the use of the Enneagram has become popular in evangelical churches and institutions.

Rohr's Influence on Enneagram Author Ian Cron

Ian Morgan Cron first encountered the Enneagram while on a weekend retreat as a seminary student in the early 1990s, when he came across Richard Rohr's book *Discovering the Enneagram: An Ancient Tool for a New Spiritual Journey*.[2] He describes Rohr's influence on him as a graduate student pursuing a counseling degree at Denver Seminary:

> In it [*Discovering the Enneagram*] Rohr describes the traits and underlying motivations that drive each of the Enneagram's basic personality types. Based on my life experience and what I'd learned in my training to become a counselor, Rohr's descriptions of the types were uncannily accurate. I felt sure I had stumbled on an amazing resource for Christians.[3]

But one of his seminary professors advised Cron to throw Rohr's book away, and Cron recalls, "At the time I was a young, impressionable evangelical, and though my gut told me my professor's reaction bordered on paranoid, I followed his advice—except the bit about throwing the book in the garbage."[4] He would keep his "dog-eared" copy of Rohr's *Discovering* in his study and come back to it a few years later.[5]

Ian Cron became an Episcopalian priest and eventually the founding pastor of a non-denominational church in New England.[6] After ten years as pastor, Cron had a difficult departure from the congregation of Trinity

2. Cron and Stabile, *Road*, 13–14. Ian Cron was raised Catholic, but he later worked at Young Life during the early 1980s to the early 1990s. He eventually served as Associate Regional Director for Young Life's Metro-East Region. More information about Cron's work at Young Life can be accessed at "Ian Cron," New Canaan Society.

3. Cron and Stabile, *Road*, 14. Cron holds a BA from Bowdoin College, an MA in Counseling from Denver Seminary, an MDiv from New York Theological Seminary, and is currently completing his doctorate in Christian Spirituality at Fordham University.

4. Cron and Stabile, *Road*, 14.

5. Cron and Stabile, *Road*, 14.

6. Cron, "Five Words." Ian Morgan Cron served for ten years as the Founding and Senior Pastor of Trinity Church in Greenwich, Connecticut, a non-denominational community committed to social justice as well as to communicating the Christian story through the arts.

Church in Greenwich, Connecticut. He describes the situation of his own departure: "There was no shortage of confusion, hurt feelings and misunderstandings by the time I left. For me, the end was heartbreaking. Following my departure, I felt disillusioned and confused. Eventually a concerned friend encouraged me to see Brother Dave, a seventy-year-old Benedictine monk and spiritual director."[7] He began meeting with the monk regularly, and Brother Dave broached the subject of the Enneagram and affirmed to Cron that "Working with the Enneagram helps people develop the kind of self-knowledge they need to understand who they are and why they see and relate to the world the way they do."[8] Then Brother Dave instructed Cron to "dust off your copy of Rohr's book and reread it. You'll appreciate how he looks at the Enneagram more through the lens of Christian spirituality than psychology."[9] Cron took Brother Dave's advice to re-read Rohr's book, and he spent the next three months "throwing himself into learning the Enneagram."[10]

Ian Cron was influenced not only by Richard Rohr's written Enneagram works, but also by Rohr's in-person speaking engagements, which Cron attended. In 1994, Cron attended an Enneagram conference at Stanford where Richard Rohr was a featured speaker, and the impression that Rohr made on Cron cannot be overstated. In an interview with Beatrice Chestnut twenty-five years after the Stanford conference, Cron's account of the event demonstrates the powerful influence that Richard Rohr had on him:

> And let's face it, one of the things the Enneagram is really good at is highlighting the blind spots and the hard stuff. In fact, when I went to the first Enneagram conference at Stanford in 1994, the absolute high point for me was Richard Rohr's talk. It was on the ancient symbol of the Wheel of Fortune, and he said that Americans are good with the *ascent*—moving up, feeling good, achieving success—but we're not very good with the *descent*—with suffering, encountering the shadow, working through difficult situations, confronting blind spots. And the Enneagram helps us understand the ascent, but it especially clarifies and supports us in navigating the descent, which is an inevitable part of life that many of us

---

7. Cron and Stabile, *Road*, 12.

8. Cron and Stabile, *Road*, 15.

9. Cron and Stabile, *Road*, 16.

10. Cron and Stabile, *Road*, 16.

want to avoid. And he [Rohr] got a big standing ovation after that talk.[11]

A few years later Cron began teaching and speaking about the Enneagram, and he accepted an invitation from Suzanne Stabile, an Enneagram master teacher who Richard Rohr personally mentored, to speak at the Brite Divinity School of Texas Christian University. Cron and Stabile became friends and realized they had a mutual friend in Richard Rohr. They went on to co-author *The Road Back to You: An Enneagram Journey to Self-Discovery* in 2016.[12] In *The Road Back to You*, Cron frequently refers to Rohr and quotes him.[13] Cron specifically acknowledges that many of the "insights and anecdotes" in *The Road Back to You* "come from my own life and from what I have learned over the years by attending workshops and studying countless books by renowned Enneagram teachers and pioneers such as Russ Hudson and Richard Rohr."[14]

Ian Cron's Influence on Evangelicalism

The success of *The Road Back to You* has increased Cron's popularity as an Enneagram speaker among influential evangelical leaders, churches, and educational institutions. For example, Cron was a guest lecturer on the Enneagram at Fuller Seminary's 2019 Culture Care Week.[15] Fuller Seminary describes Cron's Culture Care lectures as "talks about the Enneagram, the

---

11. Beatrice Chestnut is a licensed psychotherapist, coach, and business consultant who heads the Chestnut Group, with the stated purpose of "Empowering Change through the Enneagram." A transcript of Chestnut's interview with Ian Cron can be accessed on the Chestnut Group's website: Ian Morgan Cron, interview by Beatrice Chestnut, "My Interview with Ian Morgan Cron."

12. Cron and Stabile, *Road*, 19.

13. Cron and Stabile, *Road*, 13–14, 16, 19–20, 30, 36, 152, 210.

14. Cron and Stabile, *Road*, 20.

15. For more information about Cron's lecture at Fuller Seminary, see "Ian Cron and the Enneagram," Fuller Studio. The full video "Ian Cron and the Enneagram" can be found at "Ian Cron and the Enneagram," Fuller Studio, YouTube. Fuller Seminary provided the following description: "'Culture Care' is a movement toward renewal born from the integration of his art and his Christianity. Birthed and crafted by Makoto Fujimura, director of Fuller's Brehm Center for Worship, Theology, and the Arts." For more information about Fuller Seminary and Culture of Care, see "Changing the Metaphor," Fuller Theological Seminary.

unconscious motivations that influence us from childhood, and the nine different types and what makes each distinct."[16]

Ian Cron is an alumnus of Denver Seminary, where he earned a master's degree in counseling, and he has been a guest chapel speaker and guest lecturer at the seminary's Spiritual Life Conference.[17] Cron has influenced Michael John Cusick, a Denver Seminary adjunct professor and full-time professor at Colorado Christian University. In 2014, Cusick attended an Enneagram conference where Cron was speaking and recalls the impact that Cron's Enneagram teaching had on him and his wife:

> In that workshop, I had those exact feelings—feeling exposed, feeling vulnerable—and uh, Julianne had the same reaction. And it was through that day of teaching that, that the Enneagram—I can literally say this—it changed our marriage, it changed our acceptance of one another and our capacity to love one another. So, I'm a huge fan of not only of your book but also of the Enneagram as a spiritual tool.[18]

Ian Cron has gained significant exposure to evangelicals as a guest on podcasts hosted by several notable evangelical leaders such as Andy Stanley, founder of North Point Ministries and Senior Pastor of North Point Community Church in Atlanta. Because of his wide appeal on social media and at church leadership conferences, Stanley has significant influence in the modern evangelical church leadership movement.[19] In a 2013 book review of Stanley's *Deep and Wide: Creating Churches Unchurched People Love to Attend*, Bacho Bordjadze, Missional Team Leader of Cru at Ohio State University, characterizes Stanley's influence among church goers:

> He is the founder and senior pastor of North Point Church in Atlanta, Georgia. Every week about 30,000 people attend one of seven churches in the Atlanta area that fall under the North Point Ministries umbrella. In addition to that there are twenty-five

---

16. "Ian Cron and the Enneagram," Fuller Studio.

17. "Denver Seminary Spiritual Life Conference September 8–9," Ian Morgan Cron.

18. Cusick, "Episode 15: Ian Morgan Cron, Part 1," 17:33–18:15.

19. Andy Stanley also has 600,000 followers on Twitter and 151,000 followers on Instagram, and 65,000 followers on Facebook. Andy Stanley's Twitter profile can be accessed at https://twitter.com/AndyStanley; his Instagram profile can be accessed at https://www.instagram.com/andy_stanley/?hl=en; and his Facebook page can be accessed at https://www.facebook.com/AndyStanleyOfficial/.

churches that have been planted outside Atlanta that have a combined attendance of roughly 15,000 people.[20]

But Andy Stanley's impact extends well past the local Atlanta area, and his commitment to equipping young evangelical Christian leaders led him to establish Catalyst as a platform that "connects and empowers an emerging generation of leaders to be changemakers in the Church, marketplace, and culture."[21] Stanley utilizes the Catalyst website to endorse leadership resources and make those tools available to emerging Christian leaders, and Cron is included in a select group of Catalyst-endorsed authors who are regular headline speakers at the annual Catalyst conference, which draws about ten thousand attendees each year.[22] Bordjadze emphasizes the impact that Stanley and the Catalyst Conference have had on many young Christian leaders:[23]

> The annual Catalyst Conference that aims to equip the next generation of pastors and lay leaders in the church has attracted over 100,000 people since it began in 1999. These facts are given to highlight one simple fact. Since the inception of North Point Church in 1992, Andy Stanley has thought long and hard about doing church in the North American context. Whether one agrees with Stanley's ecclesiology or methodology, he is a significant voice in the modern church that deserves a careful hearing and thoughtful evaluation.[24]

20. Bordjadze, "Deep and Wide," 326. Bordjadze holds a PhD in Old Testament from Durham University and is a Faculty Fellow at The Thompson Institute, which is a Cru program at the Ohio State University. Cru is the name of Campus Crusade for Christ International. More information about The Thompson Institute can be accessed at "The Thompson Institute," The Thompson Institute. More information about Cru can be accessed at "About Us," Cru.

21. The Catalyst Leader website is a repository of Christian leadership resources such as articles, videos, and podcasts. There are currently eight resources featuring Ian Cron and the Enneagram on the Catalyst Leader website. For example, on the catalystleader.com website, Ian Cron's *Typology* podcast is listed among the "11 Podcasts Every Christian Leader Should Listen To," and readers are provided a link to *Typology*. More information about the Catalyst organization and events can be accessed at "Atlanta 2020," Catalyst.

22. Regular Catalyst headline speakers include Ian Cron, Francis Chan, and Christine Caine.

23. Catalyst conferences are held on the east and west coasts of North America annually.

24. Bordjadze, "Deep and Wide," 326.

Since 2018, Ian Cron has been a featured speaker at Catalyst conferences, where he has emphasized the importance of self-awareness for effective Christian leadership and promoted the Enneagram as the most effective tool for leaders to understand themselves and the team members they lead.[25]

Andy Stanley routinely uses various social media platforms to promote his podcast, *The Andy Stanley Leadership Podcast* for Christian leaders.[26] He has hosted Ian Cron twice on his church leadership podcast, and Stanley has repeatedly endorsed the Enneagram as well as Cron's *The Road Back to You* to his audience during both podcasts.[27] On the first podcast with Cron, Stanley recalled how he himself became aware of the Enneagram through his daughter and eventually became an advocate for using the Enneagram as a Christian leadership tool that helps people better understand themselves and others.[28] Stanley has utilized his leadership podcast to urge listeners to purchase Cron's *The Road Back to You* as well as to complete Cron's new personality assessment test, the iEQ9, "immediately."[29]

25. Brian Dodd, head of Brian Dodd on Leadership, summarizes Cron's 2018 Catalyst session into eight leadership quotes and lessons on self-awareness at Brian Dodd, "Live Blog from Catalyst '18." Cron was also featured on Episode 488 of the *Catalyst* podcast, where he discussed "how to connect with the deepest part of ourselves—how can we do the hard work of knowing and leading our true selves so that we can lead others out of health and wholeness." Haynes, "Ian Cron." Cron promotes the Enneagram as a tool for leaders to discover themselves, and states at 22:15 of the *Catalyst* podcast that "If you can't understand and lead yourself, you can't lead others."

26. The entire *Andy Stanley Leadership Podcast* library can be accessed at *The Andy Stanley Leadership Podcast*, Andy Stanley. Stanley routinely promotes his podcast on social media. For example, On July 25, 2019, Stanley Tweeted: "So what does the Enneagram have to do with leadership? More than you think. Listen to this month's Leadership Podcast here: https://bit.ly/2S4ydir" (@AndyStanley). Stanley promoted the Enneagram as a leadership tool on the two-part podcast, and also endorsed Cron and Stabile's *The Road Back to You: An Enneagram Journey to Self-Discovery* as well as Cron's iEQ9 personality assessment test.

27. Andy Stanley, "June 2019: Enneagram for Leaders, Part 1." This first podcast aired on June 7, 2019. The second podcast aired on July 8, 2019, "June 2019: Enneagram for Leaders, Part 2." Each of the Stanley's podcasts featuring Cron provides a link to a resource by Ian Morgan Cron titled "How to Lead and Work with Each Enneagram Type."

28. Stanley, "Enneagram for Leaders, Part 1," 28:15.

29. Stanley, "Enneagram for Leaders, Part 1," 28:15. Cron has developed a 175-question Enneagram assessment called the iEQ9. It is marketed as "The most accurate and in-depth Enneagram report available." Cron claims that "even if you already know your type, the iEQ9 can give you a much greater depth of self-knowledge." The iEQ9 can be accessed at "Enneagram Assessment," Ian Morgan Cron. It is also available in a Standard

Ian Cron has also shaped the thinking of Carey Nieuwhof, another prominent pastor, speaker, and author on Christian leadership. *Outreach Magazine* describes Nieuwhof as "a former lawyer and founding pastor of Connexus Church, one of the largest and most influential churches in Canada. With over 6 million downloads, *The Carey Nieuwhof Leadership Podcast* features today's top leaders and cultural influencers."[30] The Carey Nieuwhof Leadership Podcast (CNLP) is directed specifically at Christian leaders, and each episode opens with a confirmation of the podcast's goal: "To help you lead like never before in your church and your business."[31] Nieuwhof has hosted Cron as a guest on the CNLP three times and considers Cron to be a "frequent flyer" on the program.[32] Each of Nieuwhof's podcasts featuring Cron provided links to Cron's book *The Road Back to You* and Cron's *Typology* podcast.

Ian Cron, himself a trained psychotherapist, has leveraged the success of *The Road Back to You* to influence several notable Christians in the arenas of counseling, therapy, and discipleship. For example, Michael John Cusick, former full-time professor at Colorado Christian University and adjunct professor at Denver Seminary, heads up his own Christian leadership training business, counseling practice, and marriage restoration ministry called Restoring the Soul. Cusick and his wife offer a two-week "Intensive Counseling Process" that gives counselees "real hope, help, and healing."[33] Cusick hosts a podcast, *Restoring the Soul,* and has hosted Ian Cron as a guest speaker twice. Cusick has endorsed *The Road Back to You* several times in both podcasts and recommends it: to couples who "want to go deeper in your marriage, I would encourage you as a couple making sure to buy multiple copies and not just share one, but as a couple, get a copy of the *Road Back to You* and see how it affects your marriage."[34]

---

version ($60.00) and a Pro version ($120.00). The assessment takes 20–45 minutes to complete.

30. "Carey Nieuwhof," Outreach Magazine. Nieuwhof states on his website that *The Carey Nieuwhof Leadership Podcast* has over eight million downloads.

31. More information about Nieuwhof's podcast can be accessed at *The Carey Nieuwhof Leadership Podcast,* Carey Nieuwhof.

32. Nieuwhof, "CNLP 241: Ian Morgan Cron"; Nieuwhof, "CNLP 278: Ian Morgan Cron"; Nieuwhof, "CNLP 342: "Ian Morgan Cron."

33. More about Michael John Cusick, his wife Julianne, and the Restoring the Soul ministry, staff, and counseling services can be found at "Welcome to Restoring the Soul," Restoring the Soul Inc.

34. Cusick, "Episode 15," 18:50.

Ian Cron continues to reach evangelicals through his own Enneagram podcast, *Typology*, which began in 2017 and has guests including pastors, Christian leaders, and Christian music artists.[35] As a Nashville resident and Dove Award-winning songwriter, Cron's success has positioned him well to develop relationships in the Christian music industry.[36] For example, on his podcast, *Typology*, Cron has hosted such notable Christian music artists as Amy Grant and Ricky Skaggs. Amy Grant, a successful Christian recording star with a large fan base, recalled on Cron's *Typology* podcast how she came to know about the Enneagram.[37] During the mid-to-late 2000s, Grant was exposed to various Enneagram books, but later a friend, who was "flipping over your book," told her that she had to get Cron's *The Road Back to You*.[38] Grant admitted that she ordered a case of *The Road Back to You* books and gave them to her entire family for Christmas that year.[39] She has been an advocate and student of the Enneagram ever since. Grant even "sat through a couple of Enneagram classes" but is still unsure of her actual Enneagram number. Ian Cron has developed a diverse audience for his *Typology* podcast by hosting popular Christian artists from various musical genres. In addition to Amy Grant, his guests have included musicians Drew and Ellie Holcomb and Christian rapper and poet Propaganda.[40]

But Cron's influence is not limited to Christian educational institutions and the performing arts. He has also influenced at least one important denominational figure in the United States. On April 22, 2020, Cron hosted Russell Moore on the *Typology* podcast to discuss the Enneagram.[41] Rus-

---

35. Cron's entire library of *Typology* podcast episodes and guests can be accessed at https://www.typologypodcast.com.

36. Since 1969, the GMA Dove Awards has honored outstanding achievements and excellence in Christian Music. In 2015, Ian Cron won the "Inspirational Song of the Year" (Category 14) Dove Award for "O Love of God." The names of past Dove Award winners can be accessed at The Dove Awards, "Dove Winners (1969–2018)."

37. "Amy Grant has earned six Grammy Awards and numerous Gospel Music Association Dove Awards as well as three multi-platinum albums, six platinum albums and four gold albums. She's achieved 10 Top 40 pop singles and placed 17 hits on the Top 40 Adult Contemporary chart as well as scoring numerous hits on the contemporary Christian charts. She is a longtime and active Nashville resident." Cron, "What's Your Stance?," 6:30.

38. Cron, "What's Your Stance?," 6:20–7:30.

39. Cron, "What's Your Stance?," 6:30.

40. Cron's entire library of *Typology* podcast episodes and guests can be accessed at https://www.typologypodcast.com.

41. Cron, "Dr. Russell Moore."

sell Moore is President of the Ethics and Religious Liberty Commission of the Southern Baptist Convention, the moral and public policy agency of the nation's largest Protestant denomination.[42] In 2017, Moore was named to *Politico Magazine*'s list of top fifty influence-makers in Washington, and he has been profiled by such publications as the *Washington Post* and the *New Yorker*. Moore also serves as visiting professor of ethics at the Southern, Southeastern, and New Orleans Baptist seminaries.[43]

During his appearance on the *Typology* podcast, Moore recounted his initial exposure to the Enneagram before he "started really benefitting from [the] Enneagram and using it as a tool to be able to understand especially a lot of the differences between the way that I would process something and the way that people that I work with [process something]."[44] Moore endorsed Enneagram personality typology throughout the podcast as a tool that helps people better understand themselves and each other. At the end of the *Typology* podcast, Cron confirmed his friendship with Moore and stated, "We gotta go hang. We gotta sit on the porch more and talk."[45] Moore closed out his time on *Typology* with affirmation of Cron's podcast, and stated, "Well, thanks for having me. I love this program [*Typology*]. And I love listening to it. It's an honor to be on it."[46] Although he has not endorsed any particular Enneagram author other than Ian Cron, Moore made clear that he has embraced the Enneagram as a useful personality test.[47]

Russell Moore also hosts his own podcasts, *Signposts* and *The Russell Moore Podcast*.[48] The stated purpose of *The Russell Moore Podcast*, whose library is cross-listed with Moore's *Signposts* podcast, is for Moore

---

42. "Bio," Russell Moore.

43. "Bio," Russell Moore.

44. Cron, "Dr. Russell Moore," 4:35–5:00.

45. Cron, "Dr. Russell Moore," 52:02.

46. Cron, "Dr. Russell Moore," 56:15.

47. Cron, "Dr. Russell Moore," 7:00–7:30.

48. Russell Moore's written works include *The Storm-Tossed Family: How the Cross Reshaped the Home*; *Onward: Engaging the Culture Without Losing the Gospel*; *Adopted for Life: The Priority of Adoption for Christian Families and Churches*; *Tempted and Tried: Temptation and the Triumph of Jesus*; and *The Kingdom of Christ: The New Evangelical Perspective*. Episodes of *The Russell Moore Podcast* and *Signposts* audio podcast along with various articles by Moore can be accessed at "Russell Moore Podcast Archives," Russell Moore; and "Podcast Archives," Russell Moore. The episodes of both podcasts are cross-listed, and searches by subject produce results from both podcast libraries.

to "spend time thinking and teaching on a variety of topics including biblical book studies, music, culture, and a variety of other issues."[49] On the May 18, 2018, episode of *Signposts*, Moore introduced his own listeners to the Enneagram and gave his opinion on whether "Christians [should] use or even care about it [Enneagram]."[50] Moore began his Enneagram episode of *Signposts* by recalling his initial exposure to the Enneagram as provost at the Southern Baptist Theological Seminary (SBTS) in Louisville, Kentucky.[51] Moore was approached by a student who had been assigned an Enneagram book to read in a seminary course being taught by an adjunct professor.[52] According to Moore, the student complained that this was an "occultic book."[53] Moore confirmed that "it certainly looked that way" and described his own first reaction as "are they sacrificing goats in there or what are they doing?"[54] But "I really didn't think that much more about it until several years later when the Enneagram started to become much more of a conversation."[55] In his Enneagram episode of *Signposts*, Moore acknowledged that the Enneagram "presents an approach to spirituality that is alien to, and often at odds with, the language and contours of Scripture," but he continued on to endorse the Enneagram as a useful personality typology.[56]

Rohr's Influence on Enneagram Author Suzanne Stabile

Suzanne Stabile co-authored *The Road Back to You: An Enneagram Journey of Self-Discovery* with Ian Cron, and a companion book, *The Road Back to You Study Guide*, both published by InterVarsity Press in 2016. In *The Road Back to You*, Stabile and Cron focus on helping readers use

49. "Russell Moore Podcast Archives," Russell Moore.

50. Russell Moore, "What About the Enneagram?," podcast notes.

51. Moore, "What About the Enneagram?"

52. Moore, "What About the Enneagram?"

53. Moore, "What About the Enneagram?," 2:15.

54. Moore, "What About the Enneagram?," 2:50.

55. Moore, "What About the Enneagram?," 3:05. Moore did not divulge the name of the Southern Seminary professor who assigned the Enneagram book, the title or author of the Enneagram book that the professor assigned, or how the student's concern about the "occultic" nature of the Enneagram book was addressed by Moore, if at all.

56. Moore, "What About the Enneagram?," 6:30–8:00.

the Enneagram in order to find themselves on their way to finding God.[57] After working with Cron on *The Road Back to You*, Suzanne Stabile wrote *The Path Between Us: An Enneagram Journey to Healthy Relationships* as a solo project.[58] In *The Path Between Us*, Stabile focuses on promoting the use of the Enneagram in order to "guide readers into deeper insights about themselves, their [Enneagram] types, and others' personalities so that they can have healthier, more life-giving relationships."[59] While Stabile's Enneagram book *The Road Back to You* claims to help readers find a way to discover their True Self and God, Stabile's solo work *The Path Between Us* vows to help readers navigate relationships with others. Stabile dedicates *The Path Between Us* to her family and to Richard Rohr: "For Richard Rohr OFM, Who taught me the Enneagram."[60] In the "Acknowledgements" of both *The Road Back to You* and *The Path Between Us*, Stabile draws a clear line of connection between her own teaching and Richard Rohr's teaching. She acknowledges, "Father Richard Rohr invited me into the study of this ancient wisdom, so whatever my teaching has become is easily traced back to him."[61]

Years later, on a podcast with Jen Hatmaker, Stabile recalled how she and her husband, a former Catholic priest, came to know and eventually be mentored by Richard Rohr. Rohr's special interest in developing Stabile as an Enneagram teacher is clear:

> But my husband and I had worked together, and we'd had some significant spiritual experiences. And when he left the priesthood, we didn't know exactly what to do with all of that. So, one day my husband was with the Vincentian Fathers, and that's an order of priests that has a different charism, but that is very like the Franciscan Fathers. And one day, [my husband] Joe just decided to call Richard Rohr and ask him if we could come visit with him. And Richard said, "Of course." So, we live in Dallas, and we went to

57. Cron and Stabile, *Road*, inside cover.

58. Stabile, *Path*.

59. Stabile *Path*, back cover.

60. Stabile, *Path*, inside cover dedication. OFM is an abbreviation for The Order of Friars Minor, a fraternity founded by St. Francis of Assisi. The fraternity describes itself in the following way: "In a more complete fulfilment of their baptismal consecration and in answer to the divine call, the friars give themselves totally to God, their supreme love; through profession of obedience, poverty and chastity, which they are to live in the spirit of Saint Francis." For more information about the OFM, access their website page "About the Franciscan Friars," Order Fratrum Minorum.

61. Cron and Stabile, *Road*, 231; Stabile, *Path*, 186.

Albuquerque and spent most of the day unpacking who we were, our lives, and talking with him. And then we all agreed that we were going to do that again. And he [Rohr] handed me an Enneagram manuscript and said, "I don't know you very well yet, but you might find this interesting." So, I brought it home with me, and it was like a home base, every word. I knew exactly where I fit in that system and I just wanted more. So, I got my hands on what I could, and then we met with him again, and he said—after we had talked for a couple of hours, actually, about the Enneagram and the wisdom of the Enneagram—"You know . . ." And by this time, we had agreed to be in an ongoing relationship of going to see Richard probably four times a year to discern our journey and what we were doing and whether or not we were responding properly to what's ours to do and all that. And so, we knew we had a future with Richard, too. And he said, "I would suggest—because you take to this in a way that you do—that you study it for five years without talking about it."[62]

Stabile confirmed Richard Rohr's particular interest in her during another interview with Lemuria Books years later in which she recalled her journey of mentorship with Rohr. She again intimated that Rohr viewed her as being unique, as demonstrated by the approach to learning the Enneagram that he advocated for Stabile:

I read a book by Richard Rohr, and my husband, a former Roman Catholic priest, and I started seeing Father Rohr on a regular basis and learning from his wisdom. Father Rohr was very encouraging about my interest in the Enneagram and he suggested I study without talking about the Enneagram for four or five years. I don't think he would suggest that to everyone. That was specific to me because he knew I wanted to teach it. I spent the time observing others, taking notes about how people were different from me, how they were different from each other, and only listening when others talked about the Enneagram. Without explaining it to me, Father Richard's advice paved the way for me to gain a deeper understanding of the many facets of Enneagram wisdom.[63]

During her speaking engagements, Stabile has routinely endorsed Richard Rohr as a teaching master, great theologian, and spiritual director. For example, during an Enneagram talk titled "How Does Personality Affect Faith Development" at Christ United Methodist Church in Plano,

62. Hatmaker, "Series 27: For the Love," 8:15.
63. Hoops, "Author Q & A."

Texas, Stabile recalled Rohr's encouragement to her and also praised him as an Enneagram author and theologian. Richard Rohr's impact on Stabile's life, as well as her respect and admiration for Rohr, is clear:

> I don't know if you've ever read any work by Father Richard Rohr. He's a Franciscan priest who's a prolific writer, and who is a great theologian of our time. And he happens to be our spiritual director. And he's been our spiritual director for a long time. And Father Rohr years ago said to me "You know, I really think you need to learn the Enneagram." And I said I don't have time. And he said "Well, I really think you need to make time." And so I started to read a little bit. And he is an Enneagram Master. And so, the more I read, the more I decided that maybe he was right. So, I too have become an Enneagram Master. There are not very many of us. There are Enneagram teachers and Enneagram Masters, and uh people who are talking about the Enneagram who know nothing about it. And the people who are talking about it who know nothing about it make it fairly difficult for those of us who are teachers and Enneagram Masters.[64]

Stabile has also taught with her mentor Richard Rohr on several occasions. For example, Rohr featured his mentee, Stabile, as moderator during a panel discussion on "The Incarnation of the Enneagram," as part of CAC's four-part DVD series titled "The Enneagram as a Tool for Your Spiritual Journey."[65] Stabile was also Richard Rohr's partner of choice when they co-taught internationally in Assisi, Italy.[66]

Suzanne Stabile's Influence on Evangelicalism

Suzanne Stabile's preferred approach to communicating knowledge of the Enneagram is in the oral tradition of early Enneagram teachers Claudio Naranjo, Richard Ochs, and Richard Rohr.[67] In a 2018 interview, she stated

---

64. Stabile, "How Does Personality," 2:55.

65. The brochure for CAC's four-part Enneagram series can be accessed at "Enneagram as a Tool," Center for Action and Contemplation.

66. InterVarsity Press, "Suzanne Stabile"; see also Stabile's own podcast website The Enneagram Journey, https://www.theenneagramjourney.org/.

67. Cheuk, "Path Between Us," 15:45. The Enneagram *symbol* was brought to the Western world by G. I. Gurdjieff in the early 1900s, and nine personality types were overlaid onto the symbol itself during the 1960s and 1970s by Oscar Ichazo and Claudio Naranjo. Both Naranjo and Ichazo insisted that knowledge of the Enneagram be

that "The Enneagram has been an oral tradition for centuries. Anyone who has the opportunity to hear the Enneagram taught orally by a qualified Enneagram master teacher will greatly benefit from that experience."[68] Stabile has developed in-person Enneagram workshops and maintained that "The narrative approach has a lot of value because the Enneagram is deceptively simple, and nuance is very important. That nuance is best represented in stories."[69] Consistent with Rohr's oral teaching, Stabile has developed a workshop called "Know Your Number" (KYN), which can be conducted in-person by Stabile or by viewing an eleven-video KYN series consisting of six hours of instruction.[70]

Suzanne Stabile does not endorse any Enneagram test or indicator. In her KYN workshop promotional video, Stabile states that she is "opposed to the test," and "our experience, which is extensive—even the long-form [Enneagram] test—is wrong about sixty-percent of the time."[71] Speaking specifically about Enneagram tests, such as the RHETI and Cron's iQE9, she has stated, "I have not found the online Enneagram tests to be accurate because they lack the ability to measure motive, the key factor in discerning one's Enneagram number. That is one of the reasons I wrote the book [*The Path Between Us*]."[72] Stabile claims that her oral approach to Enneagram

---

transmitted to others in verbal fashion only. However, some of Naranjo's students eventually published their own handwritten notes in the 1980s, and several Enneagram books were published, including Richard Rohr's *Discovering the Enneagram*. For more background on the oral tradition of the Enneagram, see Rohr, *Discovering*, 8–13; Rohr and Ebert, *Christian*, 18–21; and Heuertz, *Sacred*, 44–51.

68. Hoops, "Q & A."

69. Hoops, "Q & A."

70. Details about scheduling Stabile's KYN workshop or purchasing the workshop video content can be accessed at Stabile, "The Enneagram: Know Your Number," Suzannestabile.com.

71. Stabile voices her opposition for Enneagram tests at 0:10 of the KYN promotional video, which can be accessed at Stabile, "Know Your Number," Suzannestabile.com.

72. Hoops, "Q & A." There are several online Enneagram tests available, some of which are free. The Riso-Hudson QUEST is a two-question test and is included in the book *The Wisdom of the Enneagram*; the RHETI is a 144-question test, currently priced at $12, and available online at "The Enneagram Institute," The Enneagram Institute, https://www.enneagraminstitute.com/. Stabile's co-author of *Road*, Ian Cron, has developed a 175-question Enneagram assessment called the iEQ9. It is marketed as "The most accurate and in-depth Enneagram report available." Cron claims that "even if you already know your type, the iEQ9 can give you a much greater depth of self-knowledge." The iEQ9 can be accessed at "Enneagram Assessment," https://ianmorgancron.com/assessment, and is available in a Standard version ($60.00) and a Pro version ($120.00). The

teaching requires her to travel forty weekends each year, teaching and speaking on the Enneagram at workshops and conferences held at churches and other Christian institutions.[73] Stabile also offers an Enneagram Cohort program designed for those who commit "to use [Enneagram] wisdom for the betterment of one's community."[74] Suzanne Stabile also hosts her own podcast, *The Enneagram Journey*, and some of her notable podcast guests include Brian McLaren and *New York Times* bestselling author Rachel Cruze.[75]

Suzanne Stabile has demonstrated influence on evangelical Christians not only through the sales of her Enneagram books and her podcast, but also on the culture of her publisher, InterVarsity Press (IVP).[76] In addition

---

assessment takes 20–45 minutes to complete.

73. Stabile has conducted her KYN workshop for Baylor University Spiritual Life since 2016, and event details may be accessed at Baylor University, "Enneagram Information." The Perkins School of Theology at Southern Methodist University has partnered with Stabile to provide Enneagram training, and the school has stated that, "By understanding our Enneagram type (one of nine numbers, 1–9), we begin a lifelong journey of spiritual work to move beyond episodic meaning and inherited patterns of behavior to wholeness and transformation," at Perkins School of Theology, "Enneagram Workshop." Stabile's KYN workshops at churches range in size from 20–250 attendees. Examples of Stabile's KYN workshop locations and venues include Johns Creek Baptist Church in Alpharetta, Georgia; First Christian Church of Edmond, Oklahoma; Community Christian Church in Kansas City, Missouri; Galloway United Methodist Church in Jackson, Mississippi; Westover Hills Church in Austin, Texas; Council Tree Covenant Church in Fort Collins, Colorado; Wayzata Community Church in Wayzata, Minnesota; The Fountains of Bronson (retirement and nursing home), Kalamazoo, Michigan; and Winfree Church in Midlothian, Virginia. More examples of Stabile's Enneagram training events can be accessed at Suzanne Stabile, "Events," Facebook page.

74. Enneagram Cohort applicants are evaluated by a committee and also interviewed before being admitted to the year-long program. In 2020 there were over 300 applicants and between 40–45 people admitted to the program. More information about the Enneagram Cohort program can be accessed at "LTM Cohort Frequently Asked Questions."

75. Brian McLaren is a leader in the Emerging Church movement and was named in 2005 by *TIME* magazine as one of the 25 Most Influential Evangelicals in America. Rachel Cruze is an author who specializes in personal finance. Cruze is the daughter of Dave Ramsey, with whom she authored the *New York Times* bestseller *Smart Money Smart Kids*.

76. InterVarsity Press (IVP) publishes evangelical Christian books and resources. "IVP has been publishing thoughtful Christian books for more than 70 years. An extension of InterVarsity Christian Fellowship/USA, IVP is a leading Christian publisher with a respected history providing resources that strengthen the church, encourage individuals, and shape the academy." Cited from "About IVP," InterVarsity Press. In 2000, the board of trustees of InterVarsity Christian Fellowship/USA adopted a statement of theological foundations titled "Our Faith Commitments and Doctrinal Basis" and affirmed

to providing Christian resources, InterVarsity Press has expressed its commitment to making Enneagram resources available to Christians.[77] The publisher claims to have been ahead of most of Christianity in investigating the Enneagram, and has stated, "Here at IVP, we talk about the Enneagram a lot. As the publisher of *The Road Back to You* and *The Path Between Us*, we were digging into this ancient tool even before the wider Christian culture began to notice."[78] When IVP made a decision to further integrate the Enneagram into its own workplace culture, the publisher chose Suzanne Stabile as the Enneagram instructor to train its employees on the Enneagram tool itself.[79] InterVarsity Press describes the situation: "As we clamored to learn more, we brought in our author (and Enneagram master teacher) Suzanne Stabile for a private workshop for all of our employees."[80] When IVP concluded that no suitable repository of Enneagram resources existed for Christians who wanted to learn even more about the tool, it made the decision to launch *Enneagram Today* to serve that very purpose. The publisher recounts that

> we realized that we couldn't find an Enneagram website specifically for Christians. Shouldn't there be one central place to find resources and articles that help us (and others) advance on our journey toward wholeness and God? We knew the answer—and so the idea for *Enneagram Today* was born: to be a curated collection of Enneagram resources and articles for evangelical Christians.[81]

InterVarsity's statement displays its commitment to the advancement of Enneagram teaching and praxis, and IVP's choice of Suzanne Stabile as the master Enneagram teacher for its staff demonstrates her influence on this evangelical publisher.

Similarly to Ian Cron's relationships with Christian leadership training organizations, Suzanne Stabile has demonstrated influence in the arena of Christian leadership development.[82] Stabile's books, workshops, and other

---

basic evangelical doctrines such as the Trinity, inspiration and authority of the Bible, and salvation by grace alone. The entire faith statement by InterVarsity Christian Fellowship/USA can be accessed at https://www.ivpress.com/about/faith-commitments.

77. Enneagram Today, "About Us."
78. Enneagram Today, "About Us."
79. Enneagram Today, "About Us."
80. Enneagram Today, "About Us."
81. Enneagram Today, "About Us."
82. Ian Cron has influenced the evangelical Christian leadership movement through

resources, along with Rohr's works, have been actively promoted among "Christian coaches." For example, she was a guest on *Christian Coaching Magazine* (CCMag) with Michael Cheuk, where her book *The Path Between Us* was promoted as they discussed "how the wisdom of the Enneagram can help coaches and clients become better versions of themselves and develop better relationships with others."[83] Stabile noted to Cheuk that she has been teaching the Enneagram for over twenty-five years and that she "first learned the Enneagram from Father Richard Rohr."[84] Cheuk posted links on CCMag's website to Stabile's Enneagram books *The Road Back to You* and *The Path Between Us*, as well as her "Know Your Number" workshops. Cheuk also posted a link to Richard Rohr's book *The Enneagram: A Christian Perspective* on CCMag's website and praised Rohr's book. Cheuk stated that, "Richard Rohr's definitive Enneagram book is an excellent reference text for those wanting to do deeper Enneagram work."[85]

Jen Hatmaker is author of two *New York Times* bestselling Christian books and star of HGTV's show *My Big Family Renovation*.[86] She has a large following on social media and hosts her own podcast, *For the Love with Jen Hatmaker*, which won a 2018 People's Choice Podcast Award in the Religion & Spirituality category and has over sixteen million downloads to date.[87] Hatmaker has encouraged her Christian listeners to use

---

his relationships with Andy Stanley and Carey Nieuwhof. For information about Andy Stanley's influence on Christian leadership, see prior footnotes 22, 24, and 27. For more information about Carey Nieuwhof's influence on Christian leadership, see prior footnotes 31 and 33.

83. Stabile's full video interview Michael Cheuk can be accessed at https://vimeo.com/325205662.

84. Cheuk, "The Path Between Us," 3:45.

85. Cheuk, "The Path Between Us," "Additional Resources."

86. Jen Hatmaker's *New York Times* bestseller books include *Fierce, Free, and Full of Fire: The Guide to Being Glorious You*; and *Of Mess and Moxie: Wrangling Delight Out of This Wild and Glorious Life*. Her other published works include *A Modern Girl's Guide to Bible Study: A Refreshingly Unique Look at God's Word*; *Interrupted: When Jesus Wrecks Your Comfortable Christianity*; *For the Love: Fighting for Grace in a World of Impossible Standards*. *My Big Family Renovation* was an eight-episode single season series on HGTV. More information about the series can be accessed at "My Big Family Renovation," HGTV.

87. Hatmaker has over 500,000 followers on Instagram, over 175,000 followers on Twitter, and over 770,000 likes on her Facebook page. Her Social media profiles can be accessed at https://www.instagram.com/jenhatmaker/?hl=en, https://twitter.com/JenHatmaker, and https://www.facebook.com/jenhatmaker/. Hatmaker's podcast website, including all current and prior series and episodes, can be accessed at https://

the Enneagram "as the ultimate empathy tool, as it helps us listen to and treat others in the way that *they* need, not in the way that *we* need."[88] She enthusiastically endorsed the Enneagram personality assessment as "the real deal" for which she "fell hard" when one of her friends could not stop talking about it.[89] Hatmaker gives the Enneagram credit as a powerful tool that has helped her with her relationship with her husband, with her family, and with God.[90]

On May 12, 2020, in response to the requests of her listeners, Hatmaker began a ten-part podcast series titled "For the Love of the Enneagram." Hatmaker is an admitted admirer of Suzanne Stabile's Enneagram works, and she chose Stabile as the "expert" to provide an Enneagram primer for her listeners in the first episode of the series.[91] Hatmaker featured Stabile's Enneagram books and "Know Your Number" DVDs on her podcast website and even had an Enneagram Prize Package giveaway for listeners, which included Stabile's books and video resources. In addition to Stabile, Hatmaker also chose Enneagram authors Richard Rohr and Ian Cron as guests on the "For the Love of the Enneagram" podcast series.[92]

Rohr's Influence on Enneagram Author Christopher Heuertz

Richard Rohr has also influenced Christopher Heuertz, who has written four books on the Enneagram which are popular among evangelicals.[93] His first Enneagram book, *The Sacred Enneagram: Finding Your Unique Path to Spiritual Growth*, was published in 2017 by Zondervan and is an Amazon bestseller.[94] Heuertz dedicated *The Sacred Enneagram* to Richard Rohr and three others, and Rohr wrote the foreword for the book. Richard Rohr's endorsement of Heuertz's *The Sacred Enneagram* reads simply, "You will

---

jenhatmaker.com/podcast/.

88. Hatmaker, "What Is the Enneagram?," podcast notes.

89. Hatmaker, "What Is the Enneagram?," 2:00.

90. Hatmaker, "What Is the Enneagram?," 3:00.

91. Hatmaker, "What Is the Enneagram?," podcast notes.

92. Hatmaker, "Enneagram Ones"; and Hatmaker, "Enneagram Fours," podcast notes.

93. Heuertz, *Sacred*; Heuertz and Zandee, *Sacred Enneagram Workbook*; Heuertz, *Belonging*; Heuertz and Zandee, *Enneagram of Belonging Workbook*.

94. The four Enneagram books written by Heuertz occupied the top four positions in Amazon's "Best Sellers in Ritual Religious Practices" category on May 23, 2020.

not be the same after you read this book." Rohr demonstrated his close relationship with Heuertz in the conclusion of the foreword to *The Sacred Enneagram*: "Chris Heuertz, my dear friend and confidant, has gone on his own similar journey, and I am happy to recommend this excellent book on the Enneagram to you. You will find here some excellent content, many new insights, and the compassion that genuine spirituality always provides—which I know Chris lives personally and now hands on to you."[95]

The success of *The Sacred Enneagram* led Heuertz to publish an accompanying workbook in 2019, *The Sacred Enneagram Workbook: Mapping Your Unique Path to Spiritual Growth*.[96] Each of *The Sacred Enneagram Workbook* sessions includes "A contemplative invitation which will walk you through a mindful practice designed for personal and spiritual wholeness and connection with God."[97] Subsequent to *The Sacred Enneagram* and its corresponding *Sacred Workbook*, Heuertz published both *The Enneagram of Belonging: A Compassionate Journey of Self-Acceptance* and its companion workbook, *The Enneagram of Belonging Workbook: Mapping Your Unique Path to Self-Acceptance*.[98] Richard Rohr's endorsement of Heuertz's *The Enneagram of Belonging* states, "*The Enneagram of Belonging* is truly a pathway to radical self-compassion. As you dive into this book, you will begin the process of life-change that leads to accepting ourselves, loving others, and finding the connection we crave."[99]

In *The Sacred Enneagram*, Heuertz acknowledges concerns that some Christians have about the Enneagram's "contested origins" and recalls his Christian upbringing that led to much of his own apprehension about the Enneagram.[100] Heuertz goes on to praise Rohr and credit him with bringing the Enneagram into evangelicalism by stating, "thanks in large part to the great work done by Father Richard [Rohr] and others to bring a Christian perspective to this ancient tool, evangelical seminaries and churches everywhere are incorporating the Enneagram into their curriculum."[101]

---

95. Heuertz, *Sacred*, 11.

96. Heuertz and Zandee, *Sacred Enneagram Workbook*.

97. Heuertz and Zandee, *Sacred Enneagram Workbook*, 7.

98. Heuertz, *Enneagram of Belonging*.

99. Heuertz, *Enneagram of Belonging*, 1.

100. Heuertz, *Sacred*, 49–50, 29–30. Heuertz attended both Catholic and Christian private schools before studying at Asbury University in Kentucky.

101. Heuertz, *Enneagram of Belonging*, 50–51.

In 2020, Christopher Heuertz started a podcast series titled *Enneagram Mapmakers with Christopher Heuertz* with the purpose of exploring "the interior landscapes of the ego through conversations with legacy teachers such as Richard Rohr, Helen Palmer, and Russ Hudson."[102] Richard Rohr's Center for Action and Contemplation sponsored the *Mapmakers* podcast, and Heuertz featured Richard Rohr as the first legacy teacher in the series.[103] The podcast episode notes emphasize the significance of Rohr's mentorship to Heuertz: "Rohr is the first legacy teacher in this season because he was one of Chris's first teachers of the Enneagram."[104] During the first podcast episode, Heuertz cites Rohr's significance to the Enneagram movement: "You, of course, were one of the great early guides and teachers, content curators, authors of this [Enneagram]. Your audio and video, it still shows up everywhere."[105] Heuertz has admitted that he and other current Enneagram teachers stand on the shoulders of Rohr. Heuertz describes how Rohr personally mentored him and gave him hope:

> Now, when I first met him [Rohr], it was at a really, really rough point in my life. I had resisted a lot of self-care and actually resisted giving myself over to a meditation or contemplation or mindfulness practice. It was painful for me. And because of some of the bad decisions I had made, and the consequences of those catching up to me, I was bumping around on the bottom of life. I was devastated. I remember on this blustery fall afternoon sitting across the picnic table from him at the Center for Action and Contemplation. I broke down and I just wept at where I was at, and how far from my center I had gotten. And as I looked up into Father Richard's eyes, I'm not sure if what I had shared with him was going to scare him off or shock him. He just smiled and almost laughed and said, "Sounds like you're right where you need to be."

102. *Enneagram Mapmakers*, Chris Heuertz.

103. The history of Richard Rohr's Center for Action and Contemplation (CAC) can be accessed on the website's "History" page. The stated vision of the CAC is "Amidst a time of planetary change and disruption, we envision a recovery of our deep connection to each other and our world, led by Christian and other spiritual movements that are freeing leaders and communities to overcome dehumanizing systems of oppression and cooperate in the transforming work of Love." The CAC's Vision, Mission, and Core Principles can be accessed on its website, "Mission & Vision."

104. Heuertz, "Interview with Richard Rohr," episode notes.

105. Heuertz, "Interview with Richard Rohr."

And that was the beginning of what's been a really, really redemptive, transformational, and inspiring friendship.[106]

Richard Rohr has remained close with Christopher Heuertz and became a founding board member of Gravity: A Center for Contemplative Activism, which is a non-profit Christopher Heuertz established in 2012.[107] The Enneagram is a focal point of the work that takes place at Gravity, and Heuertz's non-profit offers access to Enneagram "one-on-ones," Enneagram specialists, and Enneagram workshops. Among the resources listed on Gravity's Enneagram webpage is Richard Rohr's book, *The Enneagram: A Christian Perspective.*[108]

Christopher Heuertz's Influence on Evangelicalism

Christopher Heuertz has influenced evangelicalism not only through his Enneagram books, but also through speaking engagements at various Christian educational institutions. For example, Heuertz was a chapel speaker at Lipscomb University, a private Christian university, where he introduced students to the Enneagram and proposed its use for helping them combat fear.[109] He has also spoken at Abilene Christian University (ACU) on multiple occasions, including the 2013 Broom Colloquium, an event sponsored by ACU's Halbert Center for Missions and Global Service.[110] Heuertz was also chosen as one of nine speakers for ACU's TEDx talks on the theme of "This or That," which "challenges speakers and audience members to consider how the polarization around us shapes our

106. Heuertz, "Interview with Richard Rohr," 2:30.

107. The Gravity Center's most recent published Annual Report from 2018 includes a list and profile of each individual board member, including Richard Rohr. The latest annual report can be accessed at *Year in Review 2018*, Gravity.

108. Rohr and Ebert, *Christian.*

109. "Chris Heuertz: The Gathering 1/10/2019," Lipscomb University. Lipscomb University is a Christian liberal arts institution located in Nashville. More information about the university can be accessed at "About," Lipscomb University.

110. Abilene Christian University's Halbert Center for Missions and Global Service has held the Broom Colloquium since 2007. The Halbert Center's stated mission is "To infuse missional and intercultural competence into the entire ACU campus, inspiring and equipping all students, faculty and staff to join in God's mission as we become exceptional, innovative and real disciples for Christ in the world." The Vision and Mission Statements, along with more information about the Halbert Center, can be accessed at "ACU Missions," Halbert Center for Missions & Global Service. Heuertz's talk at the 2013 Broom Colloquium can be accessed at "ACU Broom Colloquium 2013," YouTube.

thoughts, actions, and values—and perhaps more importantly, where we go from here." Abilene Christian University advertised that in Heuertz's TEDx talk, "Chris will tackle the challenge of overviewing the history of the Enneagram, discussing all nine types, and explaining how understanding the Enneagram can help us gain a deeper understanding of belonging, wholeness, and community—all in just 18 minutes."[111]

In addition to speaking at ACU, Heuertz has been a guest chapel speaker at Friends University. This small Christian liberal arts university promoted Heuertz as "an author, speaker, Enneagram coach, non-profit consultant, and anti-human trafficking activist. He is a contemplative activist, ecclesial provocateur, curator of unlikely friendships, instigator for good, witness to hope, and clergy for common people."[112] Heuertz has also been a guest speaker at Northwestern College, a Christian college in the Reformed tradition, where he addressed students at Northwestern's College Leadership Conference.[113] Heuertz's popularity as a speaker has enabled him to continue educating young leaders at Christian college campuses and conferences on the use of the Enneagram to gain self-knowledge of one's True Self.[114]

Similarly to Suzanne Stabile, Christopher Heuertz has influenced the culture of his book publisher. All of Christopher Heuertz's four Enneagram books were published by Zondervan, which claims to be "a world leading Bible publisher and provider of Christian communications."[115] Heuertz's

---

111. "TEDxACU," TED. The TEDxACU talks, scheduled for March 27, 2020, were canceled due to the COVID-19 pandemic.

112. Heuertz spoke at Friends University chapel on February 28, 2020, "Chapel: Chris Heuertz," Friends University. More information about Friends University can be accessed at "History," Friends University.

113. Heuertz spoke at Northwestern College's Leadership Conference April 1–2, 2011. More information about the conference can be accessed at "College Leadership Conference with Chris Heuertz," Northwestern College; and more information about Northwestern College can be accessed at "About," Northwestern College.

114. Heuertz has spoken at other notable Christian institutions and events such as Belmont University, Duke Divinity School, Seoul Theological Seminary, and the Passion Conference. A more complete list of institutions and venues where Heuertz has spoken can be accessed at "Speaking," Chris Heuertz.

115. From Zondervan's "Company Profile." Zondervan was purchased by Harper-Collins Christian Publishing (HCCP), a subsidiary of News Corp, in 1988. HCCP claims to be "the leading provider of inspirational content," cited from HCCP website, accessed July 13, 2020. Zondervan is a member of the Evangelical Christian Publishers Association (ECPA) which has a published set of four "General Principles and Practices for ECPA Members" with corresponding scriptural references for each principle and practice.

influence on his publisher was demonstrated when Zondervan announced that its foray into film would feature Heuertz and the Enneagram in the documentary *NINE*, to be released in theaters Fall 2020.[116] The evangelical publisher stated in its press release that "Zondervan sees film as a way to broaden key messages from its authors to reach a wider audience and is actively exploring this format."[117] Zondervan's press release for the film *NINE* states,

> Chris Heuertz is an unequaled authority on the Enneagram. . . . Through his books and in-person training, he has helped thousands on their journey to self-discovery and acceptance. With this documentary, Zondervan hopes to share his compelling vision for how the Enneagram can bring hope and compassion into our lives with an even larger audience.[118]

Zondervan's promotional summary of the film's storyline highlights Richard Rohr and further confirms the connection between Rohr and Christopher Heuertz:

> NINE follows Heuertz as he journeys across America speaking to people from each of the nine Enneagram profile types, including Morgan Harper Nichols, Ryan O'Neal of Sleeping at Last, Christina Perri, Shirley Chung, and Father Richard Rohr. The diverse guest list is comprised of people from all walks of life—chefs, musicians, labor trafficking survivors, parents, teachers, religious leaders, and more.[119]

ECPA's Principles and Practices include "Proclaim the Truth in Love; Communicate the Truth Faithfully; Encourage Christian Unity and Reconciliation; and Maintain Financial Integrity." The scriptural references and details for each ECPA principle and practice can be accessed at "Principles & Practices," ECPA. Zondervan is listed as an ECPA member under HarperCollins Christian Publishing. Zondervan's peers and competitors are listed on ECPA's current publishing membership list that can be accessed at "Member Search Results," ECPA.

116. Zondervan's press release was distributed on *Christian News Wire* and can be accessed at Zondervan, "Zondervan Introduces New Enneagram Documentary."

117. Zondervan's press release was distributed on *Christian News Wire* and can be accessed at Zondervan, "Zondervan Introduces."

118. Zondervan's press release for *Nine: The Enneagram Documentary* can be accessed at Zondervan, "Zondervan Introduces."

119. Zondervan's press release for *Nine: The Enneagram Documentary* can be accessed at Zondervan, "Zondervan Introduces."

Christopher Heuertz's influence on one of the largest and most trusted Christian publishers in the world, Zondervan, is clear in the publisher's commitment to promote both Heuertz and the Enneagram message through film.

But less than one month after Zondervan's press release for the Enneagram movie *NINE*, thirty-three men and women came together in an open letter to report and share their stories of "experiencing and witnessing spiritual and psychological abuse by Chris [Heuertz]."[120] Less than one week after those allegations of abuse were made against Heuertz, *Christianity Today* reported a statement from his publisher, Zondervan: "We are suspending any promotion of *The Sacred Enneagram* and *The Enneagram of Belonging* as we sort through information that is presented. We have also placed *NINE: The Enneagram Documentary* release on hold indefinitely."[121] In the same *Christianity Today* article, it was reported that Richard Rohr's CAC announced that it "had paused all continuing collaboration with Chris at this time, including promotion of current work and plans for future production of *Enneagram Mapmakers* [podcast]."[122] The board of Heuertz's nonprofit, Gravity, eventually completed a third-party investigation of the claims against Heuertz and "found no evidence of misconduct after those who raised the allegations declined to cooperate with the inquiry."[123] While the future of Heuertz's books and films remains in limbo, his influence on evangelicalism has been demonstrated through his Enneagram book sales, his popularity as a speaker on the Enneagram at evangelical universities, and his publisher's choice of him and the Enneagram as the premiere author and focus of Zondervan's film debut.

Other Enneagram Teachers Popular among Evangelicals

We will now examine two Enneagram-teaching couples who are active among evangelicals and endorse Rohr and his works. Although these couples were not personally mentored by Richard Rohr, they have confirmed a commitment to promote his works in their teaching.

120. Eck, "Let's Talk About Chris Heuertz."

121. Shimron, "Christopher Heuertz's Enneagram Projects."

122. Shimron, "Christopher Heuertz's Enneagram Projects." For the entire June 14, 2020, CAC statement concerning Christopher Heuertz, see "A statement on the recent allegations," Twitter post.

123. Shimron, "Investigation Finds No Evidence."

Friends of pastor Jeff McCord and his wife Beth introduced them to the Enneagram while they were at Covenant Theological Seminary in St. Louis, during a time when the McCords were experiencing marital conflict.[124] Beth recalls, "Travis and Susan came over for dinner one night and brought a book they thought might be helpful for us to understand not only *why* we do what we do, but also how we could apply grace and forgiveness to all of life. It was Richard Rohr's book *The Enneagram: A Christian Perspective.*"[125] Beth's interest in the Enneagram was more intense than her husband's. She remembers that "Jeff skimmed through the Enneagram book [Rohr's *The Enneagram: A Christian Perspective*] . . . and I *devoured* it. I dove in because it offered me something I was desperately seeking from the Lord: clarity for my internal world."[126]

Jeff and Beth McCord later founded *Your Enneagram Coach* in order to provide Enneagram resources to individuals, couples, and groups with the stated mission "to help people see themselves with astonishing clarity, so they can break free from limiting patterns and experience freedom in Christ."[127] The McCords offer Enneagram certification and courses, personal coaching, and Enneagram retreats, and they have published *The Enneagram Collection*, a series of nine booklets for every Enneagram type, which "are broken down into 21 daily readings, helping you unpack your story using the powerful tool of the Gospel-centered Enneagram."[128] In 2020, they published *Becoming Us: Using the Enneagram to Create a Thriving Gospel-Centered Marriage* and developed an entire *Becoming Us* custom online platform for delivering marriage assessments and courses aimed "to improve your marriage based on the Enneagram and the Gospel."[129]

The McCords indicated their connection with Enneagram author Ian Cron by obtaining his written endorsement of *Becoming Us*, but they also secured a back-cover endorsement for *Becoming Us* from Matt Chandler and his wife Lauren.[130] As Lead Pastor of The Village Church, president of

124. McCord and McCord, *Becoming Us*, 25–30.

125. McCord and McCord, *Becoming Us*, 29.

126. McCord and McCord, *Becoming Us*, 29.

127. "Founders of Your Enneagram Coach," Your Enneagram Coach.

128. For more about the resources and services provided by Your Enneagram Coach, see "Online Enneagram Courses"; McCord, *Enneagram Collection*.

129. McCord and McCord, *Becoming Us*. For more information about the resources available on the Becoming Us platform, see "Becoming Us: Self-Paced Marriage Course," Your Enneagram Coach.

130. McCord and McCord, *Becoming Us*, "Endorsements for Becoming Us." Ian Cron

the Acts 29 Network, a popular author, and a speaker within the Southern Baptist Convention, Matt Chandler exerts much influence on evangelicalism and its leaders.[131] The McCords substantiated a commitment to Richard Rohr's teaching by including his work, *The Enneagram: A Christian Perspective*, in their list of "Christian Perspective" references in *Becoming Us*.[132] And the McCords also listed Ian Cron, Suzanne Stabile, and Christopher Heuertz among "Our Enneagram Teachers and Coaches," saying, "Thank you for all you have done ahead of us."[133]

Another couple who are active in promoting and teaching the Enneagram among evangelical Christians are Drs. Bill and Kristi Gaultiere. Bill Gaultiere, PhD, is a former pastor and Christian psychologist, and his wife Kristi is a licensed psychotherapist who mentors women pastors and pastors' wives.[134] Together they founded Soul Shepherding in Irvine, California, where they offer coaching, counseling, and a two-year Soul Shepherding Institute program and Certificate in Spiritual Direction.[135] The Gaultieres strongly endorse and recommend Richard Rohr, and during a 2017 Enneagram training session for Saddleback Church pastors,[136] Bill Gaultiere referred to Richard Rohr by name as "a great Christian teacher" and "a very wise teacher."[137] Gaultiere also stated that Richard Rohr's "book

---

and Matt and Lauren Chandler's endorsements are located on the back cover of *Becoming Us*. Cron's endorsement reads "The McCord's have written *Becoming Us* as an insightful resource for those who want to understand themselves, their spouse, and their marriage through the lens of faith and the tool of the Enneagram." Matt and Lauren Chandler's back cover endorsement of *Becoming Us* states that "Beth and Jeff show us how understanding each other's Core Fear, Desire, Weakness, and Longings in light of the gospel can help us communicate with, and love one another, well."

131. More information about The Village Church and its staff can be accessed at "Staff," The Village Church.. On its website, Acts 29 describes itself as "a family of church-planting churches that stands in the tradition of historic evangelical confessionalism." For more information about the Acts 29 network, see "About," Acts 29. Matt Chandler has written several popular Christian books, including *The Mingling of Souls: God's Design for Love, Marriage, Sex, and Redemption; Family Discipleship: Leading Your Home Through Time, Moments, and Milestones; The Explicit Gospel.*

132. McCord and McCord, *Becoming Us*, 228.

133. McCord and McCord, *Becoming Us*, 218.

134. "About Us," Soul Shepherding.

135. "About Us," Soul Shepherding.

136. "Our Pastor," Saddleback Church. Saddleback Church is a large multi-site church in California. Founding Pastor Rick Warren is a bestselling author, speaker, and recognized "pastor of pastors." His bestselling books include *The Purpose Driven Life.*

137. "The Enneagram: Sin, Emotions, and Jesus," video of Bill Gaultiere teaching

on the Enneagram is the best" and that he has read Rohr's book and found it to be very helpful.[138] The Gaultieres have also included Richard Rohr's book *Falling Upward: A Spirituality for the Two Halves of Life* on the Soul Shepherding Institute Certificate Reading List, and this demonstrates their promotion of Richard Rohr and his Enneagram works in a large evangelical context.[139]

Conclusion

The personal relationships that Richard Rohr established with Enneagram authors Ian Cron, Suzanne Stabile, and Christopher Heuertz have provided a means through which the Enneagram has gained visibility and popularity among evangelicals. These three Enneagram authors have continued to build upon the success of their written works to expand their influence in the specific areas of Christian education, Christian leadership development, and even Christian film production.

Ian Cron has developed a platform for promoting and teaching the Enneagram to evangelical pastors and leaders through the Christian leadership ministries of Andy Stanley and Carey Nieuwhof. Suzanne Stabile has chosen to maintain the oral tradition of teaching the Enneagram, developing a weekend workshop model for churches and conferences. Stabile has also influenced the culture of evangelical publisher InterVarsity Press (IVP) through her personal Enneagram workshops for IVP employees. Christopher Heuertz has become popular among young Christian leaders as a featured speaker at evangelical colleges and continues to publish best-selling Enneagram books. Heuertz's influence on evangelical publisher Zondervan is evident in the publisher's choice of Heuertz as its headline author for an expansion into film. In addition, although they were not personally mentored by Richard Rohr, couples Beth and Jim McCord, along with Bill and Kristi Gaultiere, have developed Enneagram training and resources that both endorse and promote Richard Rohr's works.

---

twenty-five Saddleback pastors on October 13, 2017, can be viewed at Soul Shepherding, YouTube video. Gaultiere endorses Richard Rohr as a "great Christian teacher" at 12:45 and as "a very wise teacher" at around 12:58.

138. "The Enneagram: Sin, Emotions, and Jesus," 13:03.

139. Rohr, *Falling Upward*. The "Soul Shepherding Institute Certificate Reading List" can be accessed at SoulShepherding.org.

The acceptance of these Enneagram authors and the application of their works by evangelicals has allowed the term and concept of a good True Self to be adopted as the self-knowledge objective for Enneagram practitioners. But as demonstrated in chapters 2 and 3, the concept of a good True Self rests on a panentheistic theology that is in conflict with an orthodox evangelical theology and anthropology. Chapter 3 also showed that Rohr's perennial philosophy, which embraces multiple paths to God, is antithetical to an orthodox evangelical doctrine of the exclusivity of salvation through repentance and faith in the God-Man, Jesus.

Why should evangelicalism embrace *anything* that carries a theological warning label? Is it wise for evangelical leaders to endorse any type of system that is based on an antithetical theology and anthropology—which Richard Rohr and the authors he influenced have demonstrated in their Enneagram works? For example, Liberty University, one of the world's largest Christian universities, claims that its *Convocation* is the largest weekly gathering of Christian students in North America, and in August 2019 the event featured the late Darrin Patrick and his wife Amie, who gave an hour-long explanation and endorsement of the Enneagram.[140] During a question-and-answer period at the end of the talk, the Patricks were asked to recommend one single resource, and Darrin Patrick replied that Ian Cron and Suzanne Stabile's *The Road Back to You* is the "clearest and most popular" Enneagram resource available.[141] Ironically, Patrick's endorsement of Cron and Stabile's Enneagram book included a warning to the audience of students to "be careful" because Cron and Stabile are "panentheists who use Christian language."[142] Patrick even further explained the distinction between pantheism and panentheism. This raises the question of whether it is prudent and ethical for Christian leaders and institutions to endorse the Enneagram as useful to Christians if it carries such a dangerous theological warning label.

Similarly, Russell Moore has used his website and podcast platform to endorse the Enneagram but has also agreed that "the Enneagram presents an approach to spirituality that is alien to, and often at odds with, the

---

140. Liberty University, "Darrin & Amie Patrick: Enneagram." Darin Patrick died on May 7, 2020. His death was ruled a suicide.

141. Liberty University, "Darrin & Amie Patrick: Enneagram." Darrin Patrick's endorsement of Cron and Stabile's *Road*, along with a warning against their panentheism, occurs at 1:02:00–1:02:35 of the video.

142. Liberty University, "Darrin & Amie Patrick: Enneagram."

language and contours of Scripture."[143] Moore even acknowledged that "New Agey things" and "Jungian sorts of archetypes" are present in Enneagram writings before warning people who do not know how to weed out those ideas *not* to read Enneagram materials.[144] This is confusing. Why would a leader in a major evangelical denomination widely endorse something with so many theological red flags attached to it? Further, is it realistic to expect an average Christian student, church member, or pastor to recognize and dismiss the New Age and Jungian components of a faulty system?

We will now identify some of the dangers to evangelical Christianity that are embedded in the use of the Enneagram and then offer some conclusions and areas for further research.

143. Moore, "What About the Enneagram?," 6:30–8:00.
144. Moore, "What About the Enneagram?," 6:30–8:00.

5

Implications and Warnings for the Church

Analysis and discussion of the underlying theology and anthropology associated with the Enneagram is relevant for twenty-first-century evangelical Christians. Many evangelical Christians have accepted the Enneagram as an ancient personality typing tool that claims to provide spiritual wisdom. Richard Rohr, a Catholic priest and popular Enneagram author and speaker, has influenced best-selling Enneagram writers who are popular among evangelicals. Therefore, Rohr's theological and anthropological beliefs cannot be disconnected from the Enneagram.

Based on Richard Rohr's theology and anthropology, evangelical Christians should have concerns about using the Enneagram and recognize that use of the Enneagram can lead to a non-Christian way of viewing man and understanding man's problems.

Richard Rohr has taught a panentheistic theology based on his belief that the first of multiple incarnations occurred at creation. He has maintained that at creation God universally indwelled all things, including mankind, and therefore all things are divine in nature. But representative orthodox evangelical theologians affirm that the incarnation occurred only once and was limited to the person of Jesus of Nazareth. Rohr's doctrine of God indwelling all of creation is also contrary to the orthodox Christian theological position that God is holy and separate from all of creation. Richard Rohr's doctrine of incarnation is not supported by Scripture and is therefore contrary to orthodox evangelical theology.

Richard Rohr has also appealed to several passages from the Bible to support his doctrine that mankind has been "in Christ" since creation, and he interprets those passages as providing evidence for a universal salvation that has already occurred. But an evaluation of those same passages by representative evangelical commentators reveals that Rohr's interpretation of "in Christ" is contrary to orthodox Christian theology, which confirms that *no* universal act of salvation coincided with the act of creation. An orthodox evangelical theology not only clarifies that being "in Christ" is a status reserved for repentant sinners who place faith in the Person and work of the resurrected incarnate Jesus, but it also invalidates Rohr's claim that all of humanity has been "in Christ" since creation. Richard Rohr's interpretation of "in Christ" conflicts with an orthodox evangelical theology and must therefore be rejected.

Richard Rohr couples his all-inclusive interpretation of "in Christ" with his premise of a first incarnation occurring at creation, and this combination produces an anthropological presupposition that man has a good True Self that has existed since creation. Rohr teaches that although God indwells all of creation, it can possibly *appear* to man that he is separated from God. Rohr attempts to establish the existence of a good True Self by rejecting original sin as a faulty and burdensome mental construct that originated with Augustine in the fifth century. Rohr characterizes this problem of separation from God as existing only in man's mind, and according to Rohr and the Enneagram authors he influenced, man's most pressing need is to discover his good True Self. In opposition to the good True Self portrayed in Rohr's theological and Enneagram works, orthodox evangelical doctrine points to the reality of man's depraved nature and original sin as necessary components of a biblical anthropology. Scripture does not support Richard Rohr's doctrine of man's good divine nature; therefore, it is contrary to orthodox evangelical theology.

Richard Rohr claims that the Enneagram is the most useful Christian tool for helping people discover their good True Self, which has existed since creation. Enneagram authors Ian Cron, Suzanne Stabile, and Christopher Heuertz agree with Richard Rohr and adopt the term True Self as the self-knowledge target, attainable by using the Enneagram to facilitate one's individual journey to self-discovery. The underlying anthropological premise is that man's True Self is divine in nature and origin and that man's biggest need is to discover his good True Self. But orthodox Christianity maintains that the Bible is the inspired, authoritative Word of God and recognizes it as the source of absolute truth. Sinful tendencies among Christ followers cannot be fully revealed by an Enneagram questionnaire or workshop, but only through biblical counsel in combination with the application of God's truth as revealed in Scripture.

Richard Rohr has also taught a perennialism that acknowledges and endorses multiple paths to God, and Rohr and the authors who he has mentored recognize the Enneagram as representative of nine "faces" of or paths to God. In addition to his own perennial philosophy of multiple paths to God, Rohr has emphasized that no single religion or group can claim to have knowledge of an exclusive way of salvation for man. This is inconsistent with Christianity's core doctrine of salvation in Christ alone. By appealing directly to Scripture, it has been demonstrated that Rohr's pluralistic perennialism stands in conflict with the biblical claim of the God-Man Jesus, who declared himself to be the exclusive way of salvation for man.[1] Further, Rohr's endorsement of multiple paths to God is also contradicted by the claim of the Apostle Peter that salvation for man is available only through the Person of Jesus.[2] Richard Rohr's claim that multiple paths exist to God is antithetical to the Christian message of salvation through Christ alone.

Richard Rohr's personal mentoring relationships with Enneagram authors Ian Cron, Suzanne Stabile, and Christopher Heuertz have proven to be foundational in popularizing the Enneagram and the term True Self at evangelical colleges, in Christian leadership ministries, and within historically evangelical publishers. As Cron, Stabile, and Heuertz have continued to build upon the success of their written works, and as the Enneagram has gained acceptance from younger evangelical leaders, Rohr's panentheism has established a beachhead among emergent and progressive Christian leaders from which to infiltrate the church. The acceptance of these Enneagram authors and the application of their works by evangelicals has allowed the term and concept of a good True Self to be adopted as the self-knowledge objective for Enneagram practitioners.

Uncertainty now exists about whether using the Enneagram and referring to it as a Christian tool for personality typing is appropriate. But if the Enneagram is truly a tool that is consistently compatible with orthodox

---

1. In John 14:6, Jesus proclaims, "I am the way, the truth, and the life. No one comes to the Father except through me."

2. In Acts 4:12, Peter states, "there is no other name [than Jesus] under heaven given among men by which we must be saved."

Christian doctrine, why do even its evangelical proponents attach caveats and theological warning labels to its use? What are the potential dangers to evangelicalism?

Implications for the Church

Would it be reasonable for an evangelical seminary to affirm that "humanity has never been separate from God" or "the only thing that separates you from God is *the thought* that you are separate from God"?[3] Could an elder of an evangelical church proclaim from a pulpit that "the first incarnation was the moment described in Genesis 1, when God joined in unity with the physical universe"—or that "the incarnation is not *only* 'God becoming Jesus'"—and *not* be labeled a heretic or called to account for his teaching by his own congregation?[4] Further, would the documented source of any such heretical theological statements be considered trustworthy to provide dependable theological direction in an evangelical institution? The answer should be a resounding No! And yet the panentheistic theological foundations upon which the Enneagram rests have crept in unchecked to Christian churches and institutions. Have pastors, administrators, and other evangelical leaders done their due diligence on the Enneagram and connected Richard Rohr's anti-Christian theology and anthropology to this popular personality typology?

This book has provided a theological context for some of the dangers associated with this modern personality typology that is now accepted and propagated by evangelicals as a Christian tool. As a self-knowledge system, the Enneagram inevitably promotes and magnifies self over God. First, the Enneagram promotes *a dangerous shift in focus*. The adoption of the Enneagram and its associated language, specifically the term True Self, can create a dangerous theological shift in focus *away from* discovering the holiness of the God of the Bible and the corresponding sinfulness of man. This dangerous shift in focus continues *toward* man's attempt to discover his mythical good, divine nature in the form of a self-assigned, man-made personality label. This is a mistaken characterization of man as good, only in need of a subjective solution of self-discovery, breeding a self-centered infatuation with learning more about one's self as defined by others. The Enneagram's underlying theology and anthropology establish a trajectory

3. Rohr, *Universal*, 43, 44, 80.

4. Rohr, *Universal*, 13.

away from man's realization of his own sinfulness and God's holiness found throughout the Bible (Isa 6:1–5; Luke 5:8). One of the main dangers associated with the Enneagram is an unbiblical perspective absent of the Holy Spirit and the Bible to provide the connection required to enable a true understanding of ourselves. A biblical self-awareness can come only from an understanding and application of Scripture's truths.

Second, using the Enneagram personality typology has an associated danger of *mischaracterizing man's problem*. The Enneagram shifts the focus away from a holy God and sinful man, and the fall of man progresses easily to something that is *not* characterized as rebellion against a holy God. Because the Enneagram makes light of sin by not recognizing it as an offense against a Holy Creator, it can conveniently explain man's problem as his lost connection with his own original good True Self. By misidentifying man's problem as one of mistaken identity instead of total depravity, Enneagram authors promote a self-knowledge tool that helps people uncover a hidden, better version of themselves. The theological and anthropological underpinnings of the Enneagram typology provide explanations of man's problem that are completely divergent from orthodox Christian doctrine. Because the underlying theology and anthropology of the Enneagram guides its users to incorrectly diagnose their problem as one of mistaken identity and not one of sin, it follows that the proposed Enneagram solution will be faulty, misleading, and ultimately ineffective.

Third, the utilization of the Enneagram *promotes a false gospel*. Notwithstanding the Enneagram's diverted path away from God's holiness and misdiagnosis of man's sin problem, the Enneagram promotes a defective solution to man's problem in the form of discovering the mythical good True Self. The Enneagram proposes that the restoration of man looks like reconnection with his original good True Self. But this study has demonstrated that, in spite of Rohr's own characterization of man's pristine divine nature, no such good True Self exists. Contrary to Rohr's teaching, there was no incarnation at creation whereby God entered into mankind with His divine nature.

The Enneagram teaches a false gospel that focuses on man's own ability to gain self-knowledge and discover his good True Self. This equates to a false gospel in which man himself is the hero in his own salvation story. Any solution that is bereft of a role for the Holy Spirit to point man to his need for the Savior Jesus is a false gospel. The Enneagram is unable to replace the combined truth of the Word and the work of the Holy Spirit to produce true personal change.

The Enneagram journey to True Self is a diversion from recognizing the reality of man's fallen nature and need for redemption, which is made possible *only* through the saving work of the incarnate and resurrected God-Man. Ultimately, the Enneagram journey of self-discovery makes the need for the Person and work of the biblical Christ, Jesus of Nazareth, go away. Richard Rohr and the authors he mentored have offered adopters of the Enneagram a mislabeled (Christian) tool that misdiagnoses their problem (lack of self-knowledge) and proposes an amusing, misguided path (Enneagram) to a solution (True Self) that does not exist. The Enneagram is a proverbial road to nowhere that provides its own peculiar language and sense of inclusion for its travelers to amuse themselves along the way to a mythical destination.

Although the intent of some evangelicals may be sincere in promoting and teaching the Enneagram for the purpose of helping others develop and maintain God-honoring relationships, this book has exposed a heretical theology and anthropology associated with Richard Rohr and the Enneagram authors he has mentored and influenced. Christians who hold to an orthodox evangelical theology are called to separate themselves from those who teach heresy. The Bible provides the solid groundwork to separate from those who espouse heretical doctrine that opposes orthodoxy; Scripture clearly teaches that no fellowship exists between believers and those who maintain and teach a false gospel (Gal 1:6–9; 1 Tim 6:3; 2 Tim 4:3–4; 1 John 4:1–3; 2 John 7–11).

This book has exposed Richard Rohr's heretical theology and anthropology, and his connection to Enneagram authors now popular among evangelicals has been clearly identified and traced. Ultimately, can panentheism and perennialism ever be accurately labeled "Christian" when they deny many of the core doctrines found in the Bible? As the reader considers the false teaching associated with the Enneagram as identified in this study, the author calls evangelicals who are utilizing the Enneagram to abandon and reject it as non-Christian. The Enneagram must be recognized as doctrinally faulty, disqualifying the Enneagram and labeling it as an unbiblical tool of man based on a theology that is opposed to orthodox evangelicalism.

It is reasonable and prudent for Bible-teaching evangelical Christians to consider the history and associated theology of *any* type of proposed system before implementing it and labeling it Christian. It is wise for pastors, trustees, and leaders at evangelical organizations to investigate the Enneagram's underlying theology vis-à-vis orthodox evangelical theology. The Enneagram's theological differences with evangelicalism are more than simple inconsistencies; they are foundational theological contradictions. The Enneagram is anti-biblical and therefore an anti-Christian tool for understanding man. Has this anti-Christian personality typology, with its clearly heretical theological roots, displaced the Holy Spirit, prayer, and biblical wisdom as the basis for hiring and leadership decisions at evangelical organizations? The information presented in this work serves as an encouragement to evangelical leaders to warn their congregants and students about the Enneagram's dangerous theology that is contrary to orthodox evangelical theology.

Recommendations for Further Research

In the course of this study, the author touched upon several relevant topics, but due to the focus of this book on Richard Rohr's panentheistic theology and perennial philosophy, there are several compelling topics that could not be fully addressed. The author has identified three areas of particular interest in the hope that they will become the subjects of future research.

First, during the course of completing this study, the author discovered that there is a lack of demographic data on Enneagram users among evangelical Christians. It is difficult to determine the age, gender, and intentions of evangelical Enneagram users. Across evangelical denominations, institutions, and churches, the scale and distribution of Enneagram users is unknown. Further, it is difficult to determine the purposes attached to the use of the Enneagram among evangelicals. For example, what percentage of evangelical Enneagram users apply it to some type of spiritual formation apart from simple self-awareness? One can anecdotally surmise that some evangelicals use the Enneagram individually out of mere curiosity or peer pressure to know their Enneagram type. But how much evangelical Enneagram use terminates at simply knowing one's Enneagram number, and how much goes beyond?

Second, given the documented inaccuracy and unreliability of Enneagram test results in secular applications, why do evangelical churches, educational institutions, and other Christian organizations utilize the Enneagram as an assessment tool during their hiring process and their ministry decisions for church volunteers?[5] Are individual donors or denominational member churches aware of the amount of annual funding dedicated to Enneagram training and testing of staff at the organizations and institutions that they support financially? Is there a biblical basis for requiring ministry team members to take an Enneagram test or receive Enneagram training? Have these institutions encountered applicants or volunteers who refused to take the Enneagram test or training, and if so, was that refusal considered sufficient grounds for disqualification from employment, ministry, or even church membership? How do Christian organizations that utilize the Enneagram measure its effectiveness?

Third, some Enneagram authors make passing reference to theologian John Calvin's seeming support for Christians to pursue self-knowledge. However, an evaluation of the biblical support for or against personality testing in general, and the Enneagram in particular, is lacking. Further research to evaluate the Enneagram specifically in the proper context of Calvin's statements will help Christians better understand doctrinal differences between the type of self-knowledge endorsed by Calvin and the distinct version of self-knowledge proposed by the Enneagram.

Conclusion

Personality tests such as the Enneagram are often referred to as being like X-ray machines or MRI's that expose hidden, non-physical things in the soul of a person. But such claims imply that the Enneagram can reveal the spiritual condition of a person in a way that the Bible and the Holy Spirit cannot. When we hear such statements, or when we are being asked to take an Enneagram test for a job or ministry position, we should immediately be reminded that a man-made system, or "tool," is being elevated above Scripture. *Enneagram Theology: Is It Christian?* has demonstrated that the theology of the Enneagram is undeniably linked to the anti-biblical and

5. Koocher, McMann, Stout, and Norcross, "Discredited Assessment," 722–29; Schnitker, Medenwaldt, and Davis, "9 to 5," 70–76. Even Enneagram author Suzanne Stabile has stated that she is "opposed to the test," and "our experience, which is extensive—even the long-form [Enneagram] test—is wrong about sixty-percent of the time." Speaking specifically about Enneagram tests, such as the RHETI and Cron's iQE9, she has stated, "I have not found the online Enneagram tests to be accurate because they lack the ability to measure motive, the key factor in discerning one's Enneagram number." Stabile voices her opposition for Enneagram tests at 0:10 of the KYN promotional video, which can be accessed at Stabile, "Know Your Number."

anti-Christian theology of Richard Rohr. This book has also traced direct lines from Rohr's theological influence to the works of Enneagram authors Ian Cron, Suzanne Stabile, and Christopher Heuertz—and even further into evangelicalism. Readers who find themselves defending their own use of the Enneagram as a neutral personality assessment tool must now explain away the documented anti-biblical theological positions of Rohr and the Enneagram authors he has mentored and influenced. *Enneagram Theology: Is It Christian?* has confirmed that the Enneagram's theological differences with evangelicalism are more than simple inconsistencies; they are foundational theological contradictions. In light of these principal theological contradictions, evangelical Christians should reject the Enneagram.

Students of the Bible will do well to remember that the role of invisible discerner of the thoughts, intentions, and motivations of our hearts is reserved for God alone—specifically for the Person of the Holy Spirit—per Hebrews 4:12–13.[6] Readers should also be warned that we can all be sinfully drawn to understand and embrace complicated systems, like the Enneagram, with complex explanations and vernacular, for the sake of feeling included. It is healthy and good for readers to be alarmed when they come across any system that supplants the Bible as authoritative or any teaching that is understandable only to a select group of Christians. The Enneagram presents such cause for alarm.

Discerning Christians should think about the Enneagram just like they do about *any* theory, practice, system, or teacher that they encounter. We must continue to ask, What does this system say about God, about man, about sin, and about salvation? In other words, What is the problem, and what is the solution, according to this "tool"? How do the theology and anthropology of any teaching or system compare to the truth of the Bible? As Christ followers, we must train ourselves to ask these types of questions of everything we encounter. Let the Apostle Paul's words to the church in Colossians 2:8 encourage us all: "See to it that no one takes you captive by philosophy and empty deceit, according to human tradition, according to the elementary spirits of the world, and not according to Christ."

---

6. Hebrews 4:12–13 states, "For the word of God is living and active, sharper than any two-edged sword, piercing to the division of soul and of spirit, of joints and of marrow, and discerning the thoughts and intentions of the heart. And no creature is hidden from his sight, but all are naked and exposed to the eyes of him to whom we must give account."

Bibliography

Acts 29. "About." Accessed September 7, 2020. https://www.acts29.com/about/.

Adams, Jay E. *The Christian Counselor's Manual: The Practice of Nouthetic Counseling.* Grand Rapids: Zondervan, 1986.

———. *Competent to Counsel: Introduction to Nouthetic Counseling.* Grand Rapids: Zondervan, 1970.

———. "Galatians, Ephesians, Colossians, Philemon." In *The Christian Counselor's Commentary.* Stanley, NC: Timeless Texts, 1994.

———. "I & II Corinthians." In *The Christian Counselor's Commentary,* 93–99. Stanley, NC: Timeless Texts, 1994.

———. *Theology for Christian Counseling.* Grand Rapids: Zondervan, 1986.

Allison, Gregg R. *Roman Catholic Theology and Practice: An Evangelical Assessment.* Wheaton, IL: Crossway, 2014.

Amazon. "Best Sellers in Ritual Religious Practices." Accessed May 23, 2020. https://www. amazon.com/gp/bestsellers/books/12771/ref=zg_b_bs_12771_1.

———. "Ian Morgan Cron." Amazon.com, Inc. 2020. Accessed September 4, 2020. https://www.amazon.com/Ian-Morgan-Cron/e/B001K8737O/ref=dp_byline_cont_book_1.

Andy Stanley (website). *The Andy Stanley Leadership Podcast.* 2020. Accessed September 5, 2020. https://andystanley.com/podcast/.

Arieti, Silvano. "Anti-Psychoanalytic Cultural Forces in the Development of Western Civilization." *American Journal of Psychotherapy* 6, no. 1 (1952):68–78. Reprint, *American Journal of Psychotherapy* 50, no. 4 (1996) 459–72.

Azize, Joseph. "Biographical Studies of G. I. Gurdjieff." *Fieldwork in Religion* 11, no. 1 (2016) 10–35.

Baker Publishing Group. "Millard J. Erickson." Accessed July 27, 2020. http://bakerpublishinggroup.com/authors/millard-j-erickson/43.

Bartlett, Carolyn. "Viewing Therapy through a New Lens." *Annals of the American Psychotherapy Association* 11, no. 1 (2008) 30–34.

Bauerschmidt, Frederick Christian, and James J. Buckley. *Catholic Theology: An Introduction.* Hoboken: Wiley, 2017.

Bavinck, Herman. *Reformed Dogmatics.* Vol. 4, *Holy Spirit, Church, and New Creation.* Grand Rapids: Baker Academic, 2008.

———. *The Wonderful Works of God.* Glenside, PA: Westminster Seminary Press, 2019.

Baylor University. "Enneagram Information." Accessed September 7, 2020. https://www.baylor.edu/spirituallife/index.php?id=870485.

Becoming Us. "Becoming Us: Self-Paced Marriage Course." Your Enneagram Coach. Accessed September 7, 2020. https://www.becomingus.com/.

Bennett, Elizabeth. *My Life: J. G. Bennett and G. I. Gurdjieff: A Memoir*. North Charleston, SC: CreateSpace, 2016.

Bennett, J. G. *Enneagram Studies*. York Beach, ME: Samuel Weiser, 1983.

———. *Gurdjieff: Making a New World*. New York: Harper and Row, 1973.

Bessenecker, Scott. *The New Friars: The Emerging Movement Serving the World's Poor*. Downers Grove, IL: InterVarsity, 2006.

Bland, Andrew M. "The Enneagram: A Review of the Empirical and Transformational Literature." *Journal of Humanistic Counseling, Education & Development* 49, no. 1 (2010) 16–31.

Bolt, John. "Editor's Introduction." In *Reformed Dogmatics*. Vol. 4, *Holy Spirit, Church, and New Creation*, 16–17. Grand Rapids: Baker Academic, 2008.

Bordjadze, Bacho V. "Deep and Wide: Creating Churches Unchurched People Love to Attend: By Andy Stanley." *Reviews in Religion & Theology* 20, no. 2 (March 2013) 326–28.

Bruce, F. F. *The Epistle to the Ephesians*. Old Tappan: NJ: Fleming H. Revell, 1974.

Burgess, Katherine. "The Enneagram Is Taking Off among Christians: It's a Tool That Maps Out People's Nine Personality Types." *The Commercial Appeal*, February 16, 2020. https://www.commercialappeal.com/story/life/2020/02/04/why-enneagram-type-test-popular-with-christians/4600988002/.

Carducci, B. J. *The Psychology of Personality*, 2nd ed. Pacific Grove, CA: Brooks and Cole, 2009.

Carey Nieuwhof (website). *The Carey Nieuwhof Leadership Podcast*. 2020. Accessed September 5, 2020. https://careynieuwhof.com/mypodcast/.

Carlson, John W. *Words of Wisdom: A Philosophical Dictionary for the Perennial Tradition*. Notre Dame, IN: University of Notre Dame Press, 2012. Ebook.

Catalyst. "Atlanta 2020." Accessed September 5, 2020. https://www.catalystleader.com/.

Catechism of the Catholic Church. Mahwah, NJ: Paulist, 1994.

Center for Action and Contemplation. "Articles and Media." 2020. Accessed September 4, 2020. https://cac.org/richard-rohr/articles-and-media/.

———. "The Enneagram as a Tool for Your Spiritual Journey." PDF. Accessed September 7, 2020. http://cac.org/wp-content/uploads/2016/01/EnneagramAsATool_digital_DVDinsert.pdf.

———. "History." 2020. Accessed September 7, 2020. https://cac.org/about-cac/history/#gsc.tab=0.

———. "Interfaith Friendship." December 3, 2017. https://cac.org/the-perennial-tradition-2017–12-03/.

———. "Mission & Vision." 2020. Accessed September 7, 2020. https://cac.org/about-cac/missionvision/#gsc.tab=0.

———. "The Perennial Tradition." 2020. Accessed July 26, 2020. https://cac.org/living-school/program-details/the-perennial-tradition/.

———. "Perennial Wisdom." July 30, 2018. https://cac.org/perennial-wisdom-2018–07-30/.

———. "Richard Rohr, OFM." 2020. Accessed December 12, 2019. https://cac.org/richard-rohr/richard-rohr-ofm/.

———. "A statement on the recent allegations of abuse against Chris Heuertz." Twitter post. June 14, 2020. https://twitter.com/CACRadicalGrace/

status/1272248652455534593?ref_src=twsrc%5Etfw%7Ctwcamp%5Etweetembed&
ref_url=https%3A%2F%2Fwww.christianitytoday.com%2Fnews%2F2020%2Fjune
%2Fchristopher-heuertz-enneagram-zondervan-brene-brown-abuse-p.html.

Chandler, Matt. *The Explicit Gospel*. Wheaton, IL: Crossway, 2014.

———. *Family Discipleship: Leading Your Home Through Time, Moments, and Milestones*. Wheaton, IL: Crossway, 2020.

———. *The Mingling of Souls: God's Design for Love, Marriage, Sex, and Redemption*. Colorado Springs: David C. Cook, 2015.

Cheuk, Michael. "The Path Between Us: Interview with Suzanne Stabile." Video podcast. April 4, 2019. 31:35. *Christian Coaching Magazine*. https://christiancoachingmag. com/the-path-between-us-interview-with-suzanne-stabile/.

Chris Heuertz (website). "About Me." 2020. Accessed June 19, 2020. chrisheuertz.com/ biography/.

———. *Enneagram Mapmakers with Christopher Heuertz*. Podcast. Accessed September 7, 2020. http://chrisheuertz.com/podcast/.

———. "Speaking." 2020. Accessed September 7, 2020. http://chrisheuertz.com/ messages/.

Churton, Tobias. *Deconstructing Gurdjieff: Biography of a Spiritual Magician*. Rochester, VT: Inner Traditions, 2017.

Corey, Gerald. *Theory and Practice of Counseling and Psychotherapy*. 7th ed. Belmont, CA: Thomson/Brooks/Cole, 2005.

———. *Theory and Practice of Counseling and Psychotherapy*. 8th ed. Belmont, CA: Brooks/Cole, 2009.

Cortez, Marc. *ReSourcing Theological Anthropology: A Constructive Account of Humanity in the Light of Christ*. Grand Rapids: Zondervan, 2017.

———. *Theological Anthropology: A Guide for the Perplexed*. New York: T&T Clark, 2010.

Cron, Ian Morgan. "Dr. Russell Moore on the Enneagram and Morality." April 23, 2020. In *Typology*. Podcast. 57:22. https://www.typologypodcast.com/podcast/2020/23/04/ episode03–039/russellmoore.

———. "Five Words That Could Save the Church." FOX News. Updated May 7, 2015. https://www.foxnews.com/opinion/five-words-that-could-save-the-church.

———. "How to Lead & Work with Each Enneagram Type." Andy Stanley. PDF. Accessed September 5, 2020. https://andystanley.com/wp-content/uploads/2019/06/ Enneagram-for-Leaders-How-to-Lead-and-Work-with-each-enneagram-type.pdf.

———. Interview by Beatrice Chestnut. "My Interview with Ian Morgan Cron, Author of The Road Back to You." The Chestnut Group. January 17, 2019. https:// beatricechestnut.com/2019/01/my-interview-with-ian-morgan-cron-author-of-the-road-back-to-you/.

———. "What's Your Stance? Feat. Amy Grant, Part 1 of 2." February 7, 2019. In *Typology Podcast*. Podcast. 32:48. https://www.typologypodcast.com/podcast/2019/07/02/ s02–028/amygrant.

Cron, Ian Morgan, and Suzanne Stabile. *The Road Back to You: An Enneagram Journey to Self-Discovery*. Downers Grove, IL: InterVarsity, 2016.

Cru. "About Us." 2020. Accessed September 5, 2020. https://www.cru.org/us/en/about. html.

Cusick, Michael John. "Episode 15: Ian Morgan Cron, Part 1, The Road Back to You." October 2, 2016. In *Restoring the Soul with Michael John Cusick*. Podcast. 30:26. https://restoringthesoul.com/resources/.

Cutsinger, James S. "Christianity and the Perennial Philosophy." In *Christianity: The Complete Guide*, edited by John Bowden. New York: Continuum, 2007.

Davie, Martin, Tim Grass, Stephen R. Holmes, John McDowell, and T. A. Noble, eds. *New Dictionary of Theology: Historical and Systematic*. 2nd ed. Downers Grove, IL: InterVarsity, 2016.

Delio, Ilia. *The Unbearable Wholeness of Being: God, Evolution, and the Power of Love* Maryknoll, NY: Orbis, 2013.

DeWaay, Bob. *Enneagram: Pagan Mysticism Promoted as Christian Growth*. N.p.: n.p., 2019. Kindle.

Dodd, Brian. "Live Blog from Catalyst '18: 8 Leadership Quotes and Lessons from Ian Cron." Brian Dodd on Leadership. October 4, 2018. https://briandoddonleadership. com/2018/10/04/live-blog-from-catalyst-18-8-leadership-quotes-and-lessons-from-ian-cron/.

The Dove Awards. "Dove Winners (1969–2018)." Gospel Music Association. Accessed September 7, 2020. https://doveawards.com/awards/past-winners/.

Drees, Willem B. "Panentheism and Natural Science: A Good Match?" *Zygon: Journal of Religion & Science* 52, no. 4 (December 2017) 1060–79.

Eck, Daphne, and friends. "Let's Talk About Chris Heuertz." *Medium*, June 10, 2020. https://medium.com/@daphneeck/open-letter-lets-talk-about-chris-heuertz-3ca661a58437.

ECPA. "Member Search Results." Accessed September 7, 2020. https://www.ecpa.org/search/newsearch.asp?strMemberStatus=&cdlMemberTypeID=131509%2C+131356&txt_name=&txt_employName=&cdlGroupID=&txt_city=&txt_postalcode=&txt_country=&txt_statelist=&txt_state=&ERR_LS_20101222_163345_30928=txt_state%7CLocation%7C20%7C0%7C%7C0.

———. "Principles & Practices." Accessed September 7, 2020. https://www.ecpa.org/page/principles_practices.

Ellis, Albert, Lidia D. Abrams, and Mike Abrams. *Personality Theories: Critical Perspectives*. Los Angeles: SAGE, 2009.

Engler, Barbara. *Personality Theories*. 8th ed. Boston: Houghton Mifflin Harcourt, 2009.

The Enneagram Institute. "The Enneagram Institute." Accessed September 7, 2020. https://www.enneagraminstitute.com/.

The Enneagram Journey. "Podcast." 2017. Accessed September 4, 2020. https://www.theenneagramjourney.org/podcast/.

Enneagram Today. "About Us." IVP. Accessed September 7, 2020. https://enneagramtoday.com/about-us/.

Erickson, Millard J. *Christian Theology*. 3rd ed. Grand Rapids: Baker Academic, 2013.

Esalen. "Our Mission & Values." Esalen Institute and Esalen Center for Theory and Research. Accessed September 3, 2020. https://www.esalen.org/page/our-mission-values.

Finley, James. *Merton's Palace of Nowhere: A Search for God through Awareness of the True Self*. Notre Dame, IN: Ave Maria, 1978.

Frame, John M. *Systematic Theology: An Introduction to Christian Belief*. Phillipsburg, NJ: P&R, 2013.

Friends University. "Chapel: Chris Heuertz." Accessed September 7, 2020. https://www.friends.edu/events/chapel-chris-heuertz/.

———. "History." Accessed September 7, 2020. https://www.friends.edu/about/history/.

Fryling, Alice. *Mirror for the Soul: A Christian Guide to the Enneagram.* Downers Grove, IL: InterVarsity, 2017.

Fuller Studio. "Ian Cron and the Enneagram." 2020. Accessed September 5, 2020. https://fullerstudio.fuller.edu/ian-cron-and-the-enneagram/.

———. "Ian Cron and the Enneagram." YouTube video. May 16, 2020. https://www.youtube.com/watch?v=pZEvsBVulsI&t=484s.

Fuller Theological Seminary. "Changing the Metaphor: From Culture Wars to Culture Care." 2020. Accessed September 4, 2020. https://www.fuller.edu/culturecare/.

Galvin, John P., and Francis Schüssler Fiorenza. *Systematic Theology: Roman Catholic Perspectives.* Minneapolis: Fortress, 2011.

Gateway Seminary. "Richard R. Melick, Jr." 2017. Accessed July 27, 2020. http://gsapps.org/faculty/bio.aspx?p=RichardR.Melick,Jr.

The Gospel Coalition. "Wayne Grudem." 2020. Accessed August 11, 2020. https://www.thegospelcoalition.org/profile/wayne-grudem/.

Grace to You. "About John MacArthur." 2020. Accessed August 11, 2020. https://www.gty.org/about/john.

Gravity, a Center for Contemplative Activism. *Year in Review 2018.* Accessed September 7, 2020. https://gravitycenter.com/wp-content/uploads/2019/03/2018-Annual-Report.pdf.

Grenz, Stanley J. *Theology for the Community of God.* New York: Broadman & Holman, 1994.

Grenz, Stanley J., and Roger E. Olson. *Twentieth-Century Theology: God and the World in a Transitional Age.* Downers Grove, IL: InterVarsity, 1992.

Grosheide, F. W. *Commentary on the First Epistle to the Corinthians.* The New International Commentary on the New Testament. Edited by F. F. Bruce. Grand Rapids: Eerdmans, 1952.

Grudem, Wayne. *Systematic Theology.* Grand Rapids: Intervarsity, 2000.

Halbert Center for Missions & Global Service. "ACU Broom Colloquium 2013: Chris Heuertz 'Friendship at the Margins.'" May 25, 2017. Youtube video. https://www.youtube.com/watch?v=ftBr81CMxig.

———. "ACU Missions." Abilene Christian University. 2020. Accessed September 7, 2020. https://blogs.acu.edu/missions/.

Hatmaker, Jen. "Enneagram Ones: The Reformers with Father Richard Rohr." May 19, 2020. In *For the Love with Jen Hatmaker.* Podcast. 53:22. https://jenhatmaker.com/podcast/series-27/enneagram-ones-the-reformers-with-father-richard-rohr/.

———. "Enneagram Fours: Ian Cron on the Individualists," June 9, 2020, In *For The Love With Jen Hatmaker.* Podcast. 59:02. https://jenhatmaker.com/podcast/series-27/enneagram-fours-ian-cron-on-the-individualists/.

———. *For the Love: Fighting for Grace in a World of Impossible Standards.* Nashville: Thomas Nelson, 2018.

———. *Free, and Full of Fire: The Guide to Being Glorious You.* Nashville: Thomas Nelson, 2020.

———. *Interrupted: When Jesus Wrecks Your Comfortable Christianity.* Carol Stream, IL: NavPress, 2014.

———. *A Modern Girl's Guide to Bible Study: A Refreshingly Unique Look at God's Word.* Carol Stream, IL: NavPress, 2006.

———. *Of Mess and Moxie: Wrangling Delight Out of This Wild and Glorious Life.* Nashville: Thomas Nelson, 2017.

———. "What Is the Enneagram? Suzanne Stabile Gives Us a Primer." May 12, 2020. In *For the Love with Jen Hatmaker*. Podcast. 1:07:04. https://jenhatmaker.com/podcast/series-27/what-is-the-enneagram-suzanne-stabile-gives-us-a-primer/.

Haynes, Jason. "Ian Cron: How Do We Connect with the Deepest Sense of Who We Are?" November 8, 2018. In *Catalyst*. Podcast. 39:30. https://insider.catalystleader.com/podcast/episode-488-ian-morgan-cron.

Heuertz, Christopher L. "A Community of the Broken." *Christianity Today*, September, 2007.

———. *The Enneagram of Belonging: A Compassionate Journey of Self-Acceptance*. Grand Rapids: Zondervan, 2020.

———. "Interview with Richard Rohr." March 24, 2020. In *Enneagram Mapmakers with Christopher Heuertz*. Podcast. 55:25. http://chrisheuertz.com/enneagrammapmakers-interview-with-richardrohr/.

———. *The Sacred Enneagram: Finding Your Unique Path to Spiritual Growth*. Grand Rapids: Zondervan, 2017.

———. *Simple Spirituality: Learning to See God in a Broken World*. Downers Grove, IL: InterVarsity, 2008.

———. "What Is the Enneagram?" Chris Heuertz. Accessed August 29, 2020. http://chrisheuertz.com/what-is-the-enneagram/.

Heuertz, Christopher L., and Christine D. Pohl. *Friendship at the Margins: Discovering Mutuality in Service and Mission*. Resources for Reconciliation. Downers Grove, IL: IVP, 2010.

Heuertz, Christopher L., and Estee Zandee. *The Enneagram of Belonging Workbook: A Compassionate Journey of Self-Acceptance*. Grand Rapids: Zondervan, 2020.

———. *The Sacred Enneagram Workbook: Mapping Your Unique Path to Spiritual Growth*. Grand Rapids: Zondervan, 2019.

Heuertz, Phileena. *Pilgrimage of a Soul: Contemplative Spirituality for the Active Life*. Downers Grove, IL: InterVarsity, 2010.

HGTV. "My Big Family Renovation." Discovery. 2020. Accessed September 7, 2020. https://www.hgtv.com/shows/my-big-family-renovation/a-hatmaker-home-renovation-pictures.

Hodge, Charles. *Ephesians*. The Crossway Classic Commentaries, edited by Alister McGrath and J. I. Packer. Wheaton, IL: Crossway, 1994.

Hoekema, Anthony A. *Created in God's Image*. Grand Rapids: W. B. Eerdmans, 1986.

Hoops, Jana. "Author Q & A with Suzanne Stabile." May 7, 2018. Lemuria Blog. https://lemuriablog.com/jhcl-interview-suzanne-stabile/.

Houston, James Macintosh. "The Future of Spiritual Formation." *Journal of Spiritual Formation & Soul Care* 4, no. 2 (2011) 131–39.

Hudson, Russ. *Personality Types: Using the Enneagram for Self-Discovery*. Boston: Houghton Mifflin, 1987.

———. *The Wisdom of the Enneagram: The Complete Guide to Psychological and Spiritual Growth for the Nine Personality Types*. New York: Bantam, 1999.

Huxley, Aldous. *The Perennial Philosophy*. 1st ed. New York: Harper & Brothers, 1945.

———. *The Perennial Philosophy*. New York: HarperCollins, 2009.

Ian Morgan Cron (website). "Denver Seminary Spiritual Life Conference September 8–9." August 29, 2008. https://ianmorgancron.typepad.com/ianmorgancron/2008/08/denver-seminary.html.

———. "Enneagram Assessment." 2019. Accessed September 5, 2020. https://ianmorgancron.com/assessment.

Institute for Nouthetic Studies. "Jay E. Adams, Ph. D." 2018. Accessed August 11, 2020. http://www.nouthetic.org/about-ins/our-faculty/8-about-ins/6-jay-adams-biography.

InterVarsity Press. "About IVP." 2020. Accessed June 19, 2020. https://www.ivpress.com/about.

———. "Our Faith Commitments and Doctrinal Basis." 2020. Accessed June 19, 2020. https://www.ivpress.com/about/faith-commitments.

———. "Ian Morgan Cron." 2020. Accessed September 4, 2020. https://www.ivpress.com/ian-morgan-cron.

———. "J. B. Lightfoot." 2020. Accessed July 27, 2020. https://www.ivpress.com/j-b-lightfoot.

———. "Suzanne Stabile." 2020. Accessed September 4, 2020. https://www.ivpress.com/suzanne-stabile.

Johnson, Eric L. *God and Soul Care*. Downers Grove, IL: InterVarsity, 2017.

Johnson, Eric L., ed. *Psychology and Christianity: Five Views*. Downers Grove, IL: InterVarsity, 2010.

Jones, Stanton L., and Richard E. Butman. *Modern Psychotherapies: A Comprehensive Christian Appraisal*. 2nd ed. Downers Grove, IL: InterVarsity, 2011.

Kam, Christopher. "Integrating Divine Attachment Theory and the Enneagram to Help Clients of Abuse Heal in Their Images of Self, Others, and God." *Pastoral Psychology* 67, no. 4 (2018) 341–56.

Keathley, Kenneth. "The Work of God: Salvation." In *A Theology for the Church*, edited by Daniel L. Akin. Nashville: B&H, 2014.

Keene, James Calvin. "The Perennial Philosophy." *The Journal of Religious Thought* 5, no. 1 (Autumn 1948) 115–17.

Kirsch, Thomas B. "History of Analytical Psychology." In *Analytical Psychology: Contemporary Perspectives in Jungian Analysis*. Edited by Joseph Cambray. Milton Park, UK: Taylor and Francis, 2004.

Knowles, Richard N. "Editorial: The Process Enneagram." *Emergence: Complexity & Organization* 15, no. 1 (2013) 120.

Koocher, Gerald P., Madeline R. McMann, Annika O. Stout, and John C. Norcross. "Discredited Assessment and Treatment Methods Used with Children and Adolescents: A Delphi Poll." *Journal of Clinical Child & Adolescent Psychology* 44, no. 5 (2015) 722–29.

Lambert, Heath. *The Biblical Counseling Movement after Adams*. Wheaton, IL: Crossway, 2011.

———. *A Theology of Biblical Counseling: The Doctrinal Foundations of Counseling Ministry*. Grand Rapids: Zondervan, 2016.

"Leadership: New Voices, New Directions: Meet 30 Emerging Influencers Reshaping Leadership." *Outreach*, September 2011, 64–68.

Liberty University. "Darrin & Amie Patrick: Enneagram." Liberty Live. Video of convocation. August 22, 2019. 1:06:12. https://watch.liberty.edu/media/t/1_xo6znoyb.

Life in the Trinity Ministry. "About LTM." Accessed September 4, 2020. https://www.lifeinthetrinityministry.com/about-1.

———. "Meet Suzanne." Accessed September 4, 2020. https://suzannestabile.com/meet-suzanne.

———. "Take Action." Accessed September 4, 2020. https://www.lifeinthetrinityministry.com/take-action.

Lightfoot, J. B. *Colossians and Philemon*. The Crossway Classic Commentaries. Edited by Alister McGrath and J. I. Packer. Wheaton, IL: Crossway, 1997.

———. *St. Paul's Epistles to the Colossians and to Philemon*. Grand Rapids: Zondervan, 1959.

Lincoln, Andrew T. *Ephesians*. Vol. 42 of Word Biblical Commentary. Edited by David A. Hubbard and Glenn W. Barker. Dallas: Word, 1990.

Lipscomb University. "About." 2020. Accessed September 7, 2020. https://www.lipscomb.edu/about.

———. "Christ Heuertz: The Gathering 1/10/2019." January 11, 2019. YouTube video. 27:48. https://www.youtube.com/watch?v=yRQ1YB4Met4.

"LTM Cohort Frequently Asked Questions." Accessed September 7, 2020. https://static1.squarespace.com/static/59ac73b9e9bfdfc0c67e1154/t/5e5e8a66de36f22b35a6948a/1583254118267/2021+Cohort+FAQ+Page.pdf.

MacArthur, John. *1 Corinthians*. The MacArthur New Testament Commentary. Chicago: Moody, 1984.

———. *Colossians and Philemon*. The MacArthur New Testament Commentary. Chicago: Moody, 1992.

———. *Ephesians*. The MacArthur New Testament Commentary. Chicago: Moody, 1986.

———. *Think Biblically!: Recovering a Christian Worldview*. Wheaton, IL: Crossway, 2003.

MacArthur, John, and the Master's College Faculty. *Counseling: How to Counsel Biblically*. Nashville: Thomas Nelson, 2005.

Maddi, Salvatore R. *Personality Theories*. Homewood, IL: Dorsey, 1968.

Matise, Miles. "The Enneagram: An Innovative Approach." *Journal of Professional Counseling: Practice, Theory & Research* 35, no. 1 (2007) 38–58.

McCord, Beth. *The Enneagram Collection*. New York: Thomas Nelson, 2019.

McCord, Beth, and Jeff McCord. *Becoming Us: Using the Enneagram to Create a Thriving Gospel-Centered Marriage*. New York: Morgan James, 2020.

Melick, Richard R. Jr. *Philippians, Colossians, Philemon*. Vol. 32 of The New American Commentary. Edited by David S. Dockery. Nashville: Broadman, 2002.

Merriam-Webster's Collegiate Dictionary. 11th ed. Springfield, MA: Merriam Webster, Inc., 2014.

Merritt, Jonathan. "What Is the 'Enneagram,' and Why Are Christians Suddenly So Enamored by It?" Religion News Service. September 5, 2017. https://religionnews.com/2017/09/05/what-is-the-enneagram-and-why-are-christians-suddenly-so-enamored-by-it/.

Merton, Thomas. *New Seeds of Contemplation*. New York: New Directions, 1972.

Metzner, Ralph. *Know Your Type*. New York: E. P. Dutton, 1977.

Midwestern Baptist Theological Seminary. "Owen Strachan." 2020. Accessed August 1, 2020. https://www.mbts.edu/about/faculty/owen-strachan/.

Miller-McLemore, Bonnie. "Coming to Our Senses: Feeling and Knowledge in Theology and Ministry." *Pastoral Psychology* 63, nos. 5/6 (2014) 689–704.

Monsma, Stephen V. "What Is an Evangelical? And Does It Matter?" *Christian Scholar's Review* 46, no. 4 (2017) 323–40.

Moore, James. *Gurdjieff: A Biography: The Anatomy of a Myth*. New York: Element, 1991.

Moore, Russell. *Adopted for Life: The Priority of Adoption for Christian Families and Churches.* Wheaton, IL: Crossway, 2009.

———. *The Kingdom of Christ: The New Evangelical Perspective.* Wheaton, IL: Crossway, 2004.

———. *Onward: Engaging the Culture Without Losing the Gospel.* Nashville: Broadman & Holman, 2015.

———. *The Storm-Tossed Family: How the Cross Reshaped the Home.* Nashville: B&H, 2018.

———. *Tempted and Tried: Temptation and the Triumph of Jesus.* Wheaton, IL: Crossway, 2011.

———. "What about the Enneagram?" May 18, 2018. In *Signposts.* Podcast 23:22. https://www.russellmoore.com/2018/05/18/what-about-the-enneagram/.

Moser, Tillman. *Gottesvergiftung.* Frankfurt: N.p., 1976.

Moyaert, Marianne. "Theology Today: Comparative Theology as a Catholic Theological Approach." *Theological Studies* 76, no. 1 (2015) 43–64.

Naranjo, Claudio. *Ennea-Type Structures: Self-Analysis for the Seeker.* Nevada City, CA: Gateways, 1990.

New Canaan Society. "Ian Cron." 2020. Accessed September 5, 2020. https://newcanaansociety.org/new-canaan/team-member/ian-cron/.

Nicoll, Maurice. *Psychological Commentaries on the Teaching of Gurdjieff and Ouspensky.* Vol. 2. Boulder, CO: Shambala, 1952.

Nieuwhof, Carey. "CNLP 241: Ian Morgan Cron on Using Your Enneagram Number to Boost Self-Awareness, Spiritual Growth, ad Reduce Conflict at Work and Home." January 28, 2019. In *The Carey Nieuwhof Leadership Podcast.* Podcast. 1:16:13. https://careynieuwhof.com/episode241/.

———. "CNLP 278: Ian Morgan Cron on How Your Enneagram Profile Positions You For Burnout, Pride, Cynicism, and Other Hidden Traps in Life and Leadership." July 17, 2019. In *The Carey Nieuwhof Leadership Podcast.* Podcast. 1:07:14. https://careynieuwhof.com/episode278/.

———. "CNLP 342: Ian Morgan Cron on How Your Enneagram Type Handles Stress, How to Stay Healthy in a Crisis, and the Best Approach to Dealing With Uncertainty." May 25, 2020. In *The Carey Nieuwhof Leadership Podcast.* Podcast. 1:16:23. https://careynieuwhof.com/episode342/.

Northwestern College. "About." 2020. Accessed September 7, 2020. https://www.nwciowa.edu/about.

———. "College Leadership Conference with Chris Heuertz." 2020. Accessed September 7, 2020. https://www.nwciowa.edu/calendar/events/13536/college-leadership-conference-with-chris-heuertz.

O'Donohue, John. "For Solitude." In *To Bless the Space between Us: A Book of Blessings.* New York: Doubleday, 2008.

Order Fratrum Minorum. "About the Franciscan Friars." OFM. 2020. Accessed September 7, 2020. https://ofm.org/about/.

Ott, Ludwig. *Fundamentals of Catholic Dogma.* St. Louis: B. Herder, 1960.

Ouspensky, P. D. *In Search of the Miraculous: The Teachings of G. I. Gurdjieff.* New York: Harvest, 2001.

Outreach Magazine. "Carey Nieuwhof." Outreach, Inc. Accessed June 27, 2020. https://outreachmagazine.com/author/carey-nieuwhof.

The Oxford English Dictionary. 2nd ed. Vol. 10. Oxford: Clarendon, 1989.

Packer, J. I. "Orthodoxy." In *Dictionary of Evangelical Theology*, 3rd ed., edited by Daniel J. Treier and Walter A. Elwell, 631. Grand Rapids: Baker, 2017. Ebook.

Palmer, Helen. *The Enneagram: Understanding Yourself and Others in Your Life*. New York: HarperCollins, 1998.

Perkins School of Theology. "Enneagram Workshop." Southern Methodist University. Accessed August 18, 2020. https://www.smu.edu/Perkins/PublicPrograms/Certification-Programs/CSD/Workshops.

Petsche, Joanna. "The Sacred Dance of the Enneagram: The History and Meanings Behind G. I. Gurdjieff's Enneagram Movements." *Fieldwork In Religion* 11, no. 1 (2016) 53–75.

Popejoy, Erin Kern, Kristi Perryman, and Anthony Suarez. "Using the Enneagram to Facilitate Resolution of Supervisory Conflict." *Journal of Counselor Practice* 8, no. 2 (2017) 136–54.

Powlison, David. *How Does Sanctification Work?* Wheaton, IL: Crossway, 2017.

Ramsey, Dave, and Rachel Cruze. *Smart Money Smart Kids: Raising the Next Generation to Win with Money*. Brentwood, TN: Lampo, 2014.

Rausch, Thomas P. *Systematic Theology: A Roman Catholic Approach*. Collegeville, MN: Liturgical, 2016.

Reformed Theological Seminary. "Dr. John M. Frame." 2020. Accessed August 11, 2020, https://rts.edu/people/dr-john-m-frame-emeritus/.

Restoring the Soul Inc. "Welcome to Restoring the Soul." 2020. Accessed September 7, 2020. https://restoringthesoul.com/.

Reymond, R. L. "Incarnation." In *Dictionary of Evangelical Theology*, 3rd ed., edited by Daniel J. Treier and Walter A. Elwell, 424. Grand Rapids: Baker, 2017. Ebook.

Riess, Jana. "Why Has the Enneagram Become So Popular among Christians?" Religion News Service. July 11, 2018. https://religionnews.com/2018/07/11/why-has-the-enneagram-become-so-popular-among-christians/.

Riso, Don Richard. *Personality Types: Using the Enneagram for Self-Discovery*. Boston: Houghton Mifflin, 1987.

Riso, Don Richard, and Russ Hudson. *The Wisdom of the Enneagram: The Complete Guide to Psychological and Spiritual Growth for the Nine Personality Types*. New York: Bantam, 1999.

Rogers, Carl R. *On Becoming a Person*. New York: Houghton Mifflin, 1961.

Rohr, Richard. "Bigger than Christianity." Center for Action and Contemplation. October 31, 2016. https://cac.org/bigger-than-christianity-2016-10-31/.

———. "The Christification of the Universe." Center for Action and Contemplation. Accessed June 10, 2020. https://cac.org/the-christification-of-the-universe-2016-11-06/.

———. "A Communion of Subjects." Center for Action and Contemplation. June 26, 2020. https://cac.org/a-communion-of-subjects-2020-06-26/.

———. "Contemplative Consciousness: Dualistic and Nondual Thinking." Center for Action and Contemplation. January 30, 2017. https://cac.org/contemplative-consciousness-2017-01-30/.

———. "The Cosmic Christ." Center for Action and Contemplation. November 5, 2015. https://cac.org/the-cosmic-christ-2015-11-05/.

———. *The Divine Dance: The Trinity and Your Transformation*. New Kensington, PA: Whitaker House, 2016.

———. *Enneagram II: Advancing Spiritual Discernment*. New York: Crossroad, 1995.

———. "The Enneagram (Part 1)." Center for Action and Contemplation. May 27, 2014, https://cac.org/category/daily-meditations/2014/.

———. *Falling Upward: A Spirituality for the Two Halves of Life.* Hoboken, NJ: Jossey-Bass, 2011.

———. "God with Us: Meeting Christ within Us." Center for Action and Contemplation. May 26, 2019. https://cac.org/god-with-us-2019–05-26/.

———. *Immortal Diamond: The Search for Our True Self.* San Francisco: Jossey-Bass, 2013.

———. "Interfaith Friendship." Center for Action and Contemplation. December 3, 2017, https://cac.org/the-perennial-tradition-2017–12-03/.

———. "Let God Be God." Center for Action and Contemplation. July 1, 2018. https://cac.org/let-god-be-god-2018–07-01/.

———. "Naturally Indwelling: Action and Contemplation, Part 1." Center for Action and Contemplation. January 10, 2020. https://cac.org/naturally-indwelling-2020–01-10/.

———. "Nature Is Ensouled." Center for Action and Contemplation. March 11, 2018. https://cac.org/nature-is-ensouled-2018–03-11/.

———. "The Perennial Tradition." Center for Action and Contemplation. Accessed July 26, 2020. https://cac.org/living-school/program-details/the-perennial-tradition/.

———. "The Perennial Tradition: Weekly Summary." Center for Action and Contemplation. August 4, 2018. https://cac.org/perennial-tradition-weekly-summary-2018–08-04/.

———. "The Perennial Tradition: Weekly Summary." Center for Action and Contemplation. August 17, 2018. https://cac.org/the-perennial-tradition-weekly-summary-2019–08-17/.

———. "Perennial Wisdom." Center for Action and Contemplation. July 30, 2018. https://cac.org/perennial-wisdom-2018–07-30/.

———. "A Tool for Significant Self-Knowledge." Center for Action and Contemplation. February 23, 2020. https://cac.org/a-tool-for-significant-self-knowledge-2020–02-23/.

———. *The Universal Christ: How a Forgotten Reality Can Change Everything We See, Hope For, and Believe.* New York: Convergent, 2019.

———. "Universal Salvation: The Cosmic Christ Week 2." Center for Action and Contemplation. April 7, 2017. https://cac.org/universal-salvation-2017–04-07/.

———. "The Universe Is the Body of God." Center for Action and Contemplation. March 7, 2019. https://cac.org/the-universe-is-the-body-of-god-2019–03-07/.

Rohr, Richard, and Andreas Ebert. *Discovering the Enneagram: An Ancient Tool for a New Spiritual Journey.* New York: Crossroad, 1992.

Russell Moore (website). "Bio." Ethics and Religious Liberty Commission of the Southern Baptist Convention. 2020. Accessed September 7, 2020. https://www.russellmoore.com/about/.

———. "Podcast Archives." Ethics and Religious Liberty Commission of the Southern Baptist Convention. 2020. Accessed September 7, 2020. https://www.russellmoore.com/category/podcast/.

———. "Russell Moore Podcast Archives." Ethics and Religious Liberty Commission of the Southern Baptist Convention. 2020. Accessed September 7, 2020. https://www.russellmoore.com/category/russell-moore-podcast/.

Saddleback Church. "Our Pastor." 2020. Accessed August 19, 2020. https://saddleback.com/visit/about/pastors/our-pastor.

———. *The Enneagram: A Christian Perspective.* New York: Crossroad, 2018.

———. *Experiencing the Enneagram.* New York: Crossroad Publishing, 1992.

Schaeffer, Francis A. *The Francis Schaeffer Trilogy.* Wheaton, IL: Crossway, 1990.

Schnitker, Sarah A., Jay Medenwaldt, and Lizzy Davis. "9 to 5." *Christianity Today* (January 2021) 70–76.

Shapiro, Rami. *Perennial Wisdom for the Spiritually Independent: Sacred Teachings – Annotated & Explained.* Westminster, CO: Skylight Paths, 2013.

———, ed. *World Wisdom Bible: A New Testament for a Global Spirituality.* Westminster, CO: Skylight Paths, 2017.

Shimron, Yonat. "Christopher Heuertz's Enneagram Projects Halted over Abuse Allegations." *Christianity Today,* June 16, 2020. https://www.christianitytoday. com/news/2020/june/christopher-heuertz-enneagram-zondervan-brene-brown-abuse-p.html.

———. "Investigation Finds No Evidence for Recent Allegations against Chris Heuertz." *Religion News Service,* July 28, 2020. https://religionnews.com/2020/07/28/ investigation-finds-no-new-evidence-of-misconduct-by-chris-heuertz/.

Shirley, John. *Gurdjieff: An Introduction to His Life and Times.* New York: Tarcher, 2004.

Shorter Oxford English Dictionary. 5th ed. Vol. 2. Oxford: Oxford University Press, 2002.

Skinner, B. F. *Beyond Freedom and Dignity.* New York: Alfred A. Knopf, 1971.

Smith, Robert. *The Christian Counselor's Medical Desk Reference.* Stanley, NC: Timeless Texts, 2000.

Soul Shepherding. "About Us." 2020. Accessed June 11, 2020. https://www.soulshepherding. org/about-us/.

———. "The Enneagram: Sin, Emotions, and Jesus." October 13, 2017. Youtube video. 1:42:18. https://www.youtube.com/watch?v=23DOQCqvsxA&fbclid= IwAR3lDtiD klVpGgxPG-E7NPBJmiR-0-OQ4aHIVYjkJRX0Z06Fe8qZ9-NOmgw.

———. "Soul Shepherding Institute Certificate Reading List." 2020. Accessed September 7, 2020. https://www.soulshepherding.org/reading-list-spiritual-direction-certificate/.

Speeth, Kathleen Riordan. *The Gurdjieff Work.* Berkeley, CA: And/Or, 1976.

Speeth, Kathleen Riordan, and Ira Friedlander. *Gurdjieff, Seeker of the Truth.* New York: Harper and Row, 1980.

Stabile, Suzanne. "Events." Facebook page. Accessed September 7, 2020. https://www. facebook.com/EnneagramSuz/events/?ref=page_internal.

———. "The Enneagram: Know Your Number." Suzannestabile.com. Accessed September 7, 2020. https://suzannestabile.com/kyn.

———. "How Does Personality Affect Faith Development?" Youtube video. April 20, 2012. 1:30:14. https://www.youtube.com/watch?v=mVIurb-xdfI.

———. *The Path in Between Us: An Enneagram Journey to Healthy Relationships.* Downers Grove, IL: InterVarsity, 2018.

Stanley, Andy. "June 2019: Enneagram for Leaders, Part 1." June 7, 2019. In *The Andy Stanley Leadership Podcast.* Podcast. 30:00. https://andystanley.com/podcast/ enneagram-for-leaders-part-1/#.

———. "June 2019: Enneagram for Leaders, Part 2." July 8, 2019. In *The Andy Stanley Leadership Podcast.* Podcast. 30:45. https://andystanley.com/podcast/enneagram-for-leaders-part-2/.

Starke, John. "An Evangelical's Guide to the Enneagram." *Christianity Today* 60, no. 9 (2016): 54.

Strachan, Owen. *Reenchanting Humanity: A Theology of Mankind.* Fearn, Scotland: Christian Focus, 2019.

Strachan, Owen, and Gavin Peacock. *The Grand Design: Male and Female He Made Them.* Fearn, Scotland: Christian Focus, 2016.

Sutton, Anna. "But Is It Real?: A Review of Research on the Enneagram." *Enneagram Journal* 5, no. 1 (2012) 5–19.

Tan, Siang-Yang. *Counseling and Psychotherapy: A Christian Perspective.* Grand Rapids: Baker Academic, 2011.

Tapp, Karen, and Ken Engebretson. "Using the Enneagram for Client Insight and Transformation: A Type Eight Illustration." *Journal of Creativity in Mental Health* 5, no. 1 (2010) 65–72.

Taylor, Catherine. "The Process Enneagram: A Practitioner's Guide to Its Use as a Facilitative Tool in the Corporate Environment." *Emergence: Complexity & Organization* 15, no. 1 (2013) 55–70.

TED. "TEDxACU." TED Conferences, LLC. Accessed September 7, 2020. https://www.ted.com/tedx/events/35795.

Thayer, Joseph Henry. *A Greek-English Lexicon of the New Testament.* 5th ed. New York: Charles Scribner, 1956.

Thomas, Owen C. "Christianity and the Perennial Philosophy." *Theology Today* 43, no. 2 (1986) 259–66.

The Thompson Institute. "The Thompson Institute." Cru Ohio State. Accessed September 5, 2020. https://thethompsoninstitute.org/about/the-institute.

Typology Podcast. "Typology." 2017. https://www.typologypodcast.com/home.

Veinot, Don, Joy Veinot, and Marcia Montenegro. *Richard Rohr and the Enneagram Secret.* Wonder Lake, IL: MCOI, 2020.

The Village Church. "Staff." 2020. Accessed September 7, 2020. https://thevillagechurch.net/about/staff?GroupId=431108&currentGroup=central-elders.

Wagner, Jerome P., and Ronald E. Walker. "Reliability and Validity Study of a Sufi Personality Typology: The Enneagram." *Journal of Clinical Psychology* 39, no. 5 (1983) 712–17.

Walberg, Michel. *Gurdjieff, An Approach to His Ideas.* London: Routledge and Kegan Paul, 1981.

Warren, Rick. *The Purpose Driven Life: What On Earth Am I Here For?* Grand Rapids: Zondervan, 2002.

Webb, James. *The Harmonious Circle: The Lives and Work of G. I. Gurdjieff, P. D. Ouspensky, and Their Followers.* New York: G. P. Putnam, 1980.

Weeks, Noel. *The Sufficiency of Scripture.* Carlisle, PA: Banner of Truth Trust, 1988.

Wheaton College. "Marc Cortez." 2020. Accessed August 1, 2020. https://www.wheaton.edu/academics/faculty/marc-cortez/.

Wiersbe, Warren W. *New Testament.* Vols. 1–2. The Bible Exposition Commentary. Colorado Springs: Cook Communications, 2001.

Wipf and Stock Publishers. "Truth on Trial." 2020. Accessed July 27, 2020. https://wipfandstock.com/truth-on-trial.html.

Word Made Flesh. "About Us." 2020. Accessed September 4, 2020. https://wordmadeflesh.org/about/.

Your Enneagram Coach. "Founders of Your Enneagram Coach." 2020. Accessed September 4, 2020. https://www.yourenneagramcoach.com/about.

———. "Online Enneagram Courses." 2020. Accessed September 7, 2020. https://www.yourenneagramcoach.com/enneagram-online-courses.

Zondervan. "Company Profile." 2020. Accessed September 7, 2020. https://www.zondervan.com/about-us/company-profile/.

———. "Zondervan Introduces New Enneagram Documentary from Bestselling Enneagram Author Christopher L. Heuertz: 'NINE: THE ENNEAGRAM DOCUMENTARY' to Release in Theaters Fall 2020." *Christian News Wire*, May 20, 2020. http://christiannewswire.com/news/2720383895.html? fbclid=IwAR1hEVNJrGo7fz7DoXsEjgJoA8ci7vOJLIgznSUp-s_uO2xpoNpnR4huuWc.

Made in the USA
Las Vegas, NV
17 March 2022

45816828R00085